1

# HOW TO BUILD AN ENHANCED COMPUTER AND TAKE OVER THE WORLD

## BY CHARLES ALBERT MOSTER

© 2019 by Charles Albert Moster

2

"This book is dedicated to my daughter, Charley, who at age two plus, is my template for the "Conscious AI" of the same name depicted in this work. For her sake and the rest of us, I hope my predictions are incorrect. That said, I would bet the "law practice" on the accuracy of my prognostications and anticipate that my girl will lead the charge into the future."

ZIGAMUS GLORIBUS PUBLISHING COMPANY
4920 South Loop 289 – Suite 101
Lubbock, Texas 79414

# I.

# <u>PREFACE</u>

On August 2, 1939, Albert Einstein and his colleague Leo Szilard, wrote a letter to President Franklin Delano Roosevelt, warning him of the imminent danger of Nazi Germany building an atomic bomb before the United States and the critical need to launch a developmental program. The message was loud and clear to FDR – if the Nazi's beat

America to the atomic punch, their world domination would be assured. There was little doubt that Adolph Hitler would employ this devastating technology to obliterate the United States and force an unconditional surrender.

## Early Nazi Efforts to Build an Atomic Bomb

The Manhattan Project was launched in 1939 and resulted in the detonation of the World's first atomic bomb at the Trinity site in New Mexico in 1945. Shortly thereafter, on August 6, 1945, President Harry Truman issued the order to drop the atomic bomb on Hiroshima, Japan which resulted in the death of 146,000 people and a warning from Washington for Japan to unconditionally surrender or "expect a rain of ruin from the air, the like of which has never been seen on this earth".[i]

The Japanese failed to immediately heed this dire warning and suffered the consequences of a second atomic bombing over Nagasaki on August 9, 1945 resulting in the death of over 80,000 people. Facing

the certainty of total devastation, the Emperor of Japan, authorized the

unconditional surrender of Japan which was delivered to the Allies on

September 2, 1945.

Imagine the consequences if Albert Einstein and Leo Szilard failed

to compose the letter to FDR? This dire thought experiment is

brilliantly depicted in the book and film, "The Man in the High Castle",

where Germany went on the win the Second World War by developing

the Atomic Bomb before the United States.[ii]

Without the need for exaggeration, the United States is confronted

by an identical risk of annihilation in 2019. This threat is not embodied

in a mushroom cloud but every bit as deadly. At this very moment,

computer scientists in Russia and China are accelerating their efforts to

develop the world's first quantum computer capable of decrypting our

most secret passwords in commerce and national defense. This

offensive capability is being coupled with efforts to render their own

encryption impenetrable through the same quantum technology. Such

would constitute a "one two punch" to the United States as it would first neutralize and cripple our offensive and defensive nuclear weapons via decryption quantum technology while concurrently insulating the enemy encryption from attack utilizing the flip side of the same technology.

This is being followed by work on what will later be described as "Augmented AI" systems and ultimately, a conscious computer – "Conscious AI". Whoever wins this "Computer Race" will be assured world domination. If America fails to rise to this challenge, it will suffer the same fate which befell Japan. There will be a massive loss of life of "the like of which the world has never seen" and our way of life will end.

It is the objective of this work to set out the reasons for my great concern and the need to immediately launch a developmental project akin to the Manhattan Project for purposes of developing decryption computer technology and quantum encrypted systems, Augmented AI, and Conscious AI systems. The risks confronted by our country are palpable and deadly. I would urge that our visionaries in the area of computer science draft a letter to President Trump in the same spirit as Einstein's admonition to FDR. A similar letter under this author's

7

signature is being delivered to the White House on the date of

publication of this book.[iii]

# II.

# <u>THE NEW MUSHROOM CLOUD</u>

Perhaps you might think that I am overreacting. Afterall, we are talking about micro-circuitry, electronics, and cultured neurons - whether binary, quantum, or biological. How can a bunch of data points result in the death and destruction of an atomic bomb?

The typical threat raised by the so-called computer doomsayers is that advanced computers, particularly quantum technologies, will allow an encrypted code to be broken. As one technology analyst framed the issue, "It is no wonder that the quantum computing investments in the United States, China, and elsewhere are ramping. Now that the technology is moving from research to practice, governments are banking on having technology's most powerful weapon first – one that can crack encryption and render a nation's economy defenseless".[iv]

The debate has been almost entirely monopolized by the fear of new decryption technologies which may render all of our banking systems which rely on password protected communications defenseless. Without exaggeration, such a computer breakthrough would have devastating consequences to our economy and way of life.

10

This technology would have lethal defensive and offensive capabilities. Quantum Key Distribution (QKD) uses quantum entanglement to better *defend* encrypted systems. "The most common form of quantum encryption is the transmission of cryptographic keys using quantum superpositions of photons during the initiation of the secure communication sessions. In keeping with Heisenberg's Uncertainty Principle, the exact states of the photons are indeterminate until they are isolated and measured- only then do they exhibit a special state of polarization as the very process of interrupting (or eavesdropping) qubits irreversibly changes it. QKD offers a valuable means of knowing if communications have been interrupted (e.g., through a man-in-the-middle attack).[v]

Conversely, quantum technology can be harnessed as an *offensive* weapon to decrypt our military and financial communications through a process known as "quantum cryptography" – which refers to the specific application of quantum computing for decrypting encoded messages. "Current encryption standards primarily rely upon mathematical algorithms encoding data, which are effectively unbreakable in any

development of more efficient aircraft or missile systems such as the dreaded new stealth hypersonic weapons touted by Russia.

A conscious computer would represent an amplification of intelligence beyond the human level entirely and constitute what this author refers to as "Breaking Conscious AI Barrier" (See Chapter V).

A conscious computer which crosses this threshold would be sentient and capable of formulating questions and solutions beyond the prior constraints of human intellect and human/computer augmentation.

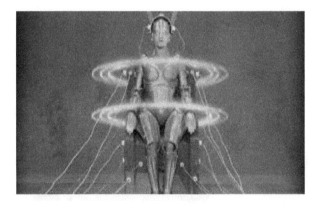

## <u>Conscious Robot from Metropolis (1927)</u>

By way of analogy, a system operating beyond the "Conscious AI Barrier" would not simply devise a more efficient aircraft or missile system, but an entirely new and unforeseen technology itself representing a paradigm shift akin to the invention of human teleportation in an age of steam driven locomotives and horse drawn carriages. Simply put, the technological breakthrough would beyond our human ability to create or even imagine.

Superficially, what would be the products of such a system? Perhaps, the fabrication of artificial wormholes or quantum entangled transference of matter which is unthinkable employing current technology. If Time Travel is possible, a Conscious AI would discover it.

## Conscious AI Could Reimagine this Classic – Could the Technology be Created?

On the biological front, there would be no need to cure cancer if all diseases were not only cured but made irrelevant by new technologies which would extend human life beyond the confines of our physical bodies.  Immortality would cure cancer for sure.

Of course, the flipside of these new technologies emerging at the "Augmented AI Barrier" and beyond at the "Conscious AI Barrier" are frightening to behold.  If our adversaries could develop military capabilities which break the "Augmented AI Barrier" capable of accelerating to millions of miles per hour and evading detection, how could we possibly defend the homeland against such threat?  Taking the technology to the unforeseen "Conscious AI Barrier", how would we defend against the possibility of thousands of soldiers or androids teleporting instantaneously to every city in the United States in a massive attack?

The rejoinder to these perceived risks is to relegate such doomsayers to the world of science fiction with Star Trek and the Terminator movies being prime examples.  The purpose of this work is to make the case that our science fiction imaginings will become a reality in the very near future.  Whichever country first crosses through

16

the "Encryption Barrier", Augmented AI Barrier", or the "Conscious AI

Barrier" will with 100 percent certainty, take over the world.

# III.

# <u>Breaking the Encryption Barrier</u>

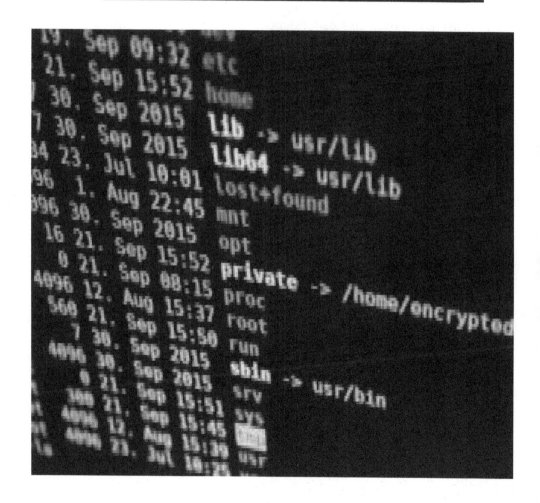

### **3.1 – A Brief History of Encryption Systems.**

To understand the risks attendant to the creation of encryption technologies, we must first explore the history of encrypted systems and our pervasive reliance and dependence on encrypted algorithms. Encryption is the process of using an algorithm to transform information to make it unreadable for unauthorized users. This cryptographic method protects sensitive data such as credit card numbers by encoding and transforming information into unreadable cipher text. This encoded data may only be decrypted or made readable with a key. Symmetric-key and asymmetric-key are the two primary types of encryption."viii

The first use of encryption has been traced to Egyptian hieroglyphics dating back to 1900 BC where the symbols were intentionally altered to safeguard critical messages intended for the Pharaohs or other high officials.

An early cryptographic system captured on hieroglyphics appears below.

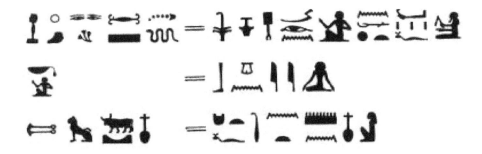

# Egyptian Encryption – 1900 BC

The first mechanical encryption systems were introduced by Julius Caesar in 100 BC for use by his invading forces. A process known as the "Substitutional Cipher" was devised whereby letters in the original communication were transposed to correlate with assigned characters. For example, the letter "A" would be correlated with the letter "D" which would be substituted in place thereof (or three places over). Thus, if Caesar was heading to Rome the city would be replaced by the following: "URPH". Obviously, it was relatively easy to break these simplistic systems, although Caesar was light years ahead of his adversaries in the use of encryption. Below is an illustration as how a "substitutional cipher" operates.

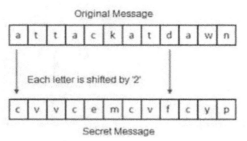

Original Message

| a | t | t | a | c | k | a | t | d | a | w | n |

Each letter is shifted by '2'

| c | v | v | c | e | m | c | v | f | c | y | p |

Secret Message

# The Caesar Cipher

The development of "encryption keys" in the 16th Century

represented a breakthrough in protected communications. An encryption

key is a random string of bits created explicitly for scrambling and

unscrambling data. Encryption keys are designed with algorithms

intended to ensure that every key is unpredictable and unique.[ix]

# 16th Century French Encryption Book

# <u>Jefferson Cipher Wheel</u>

Thomas Jefferson invented a 26-wheel encryption key system which created a random sequence of letters. This ingenious system utilized the random lineup of the 26 wheels to encrypt a full message. The configuration of the wheels constituted the algorithm for purposes of the encryption key.

As the sophistication of encrypted systems evolved, so did the state of encryption methodology as mathematicians sought ever more innovative approaches to break the code. A classic example of a successful encryption effort occurred in February 24, 1917 when the British turned over to the United States a secret telegram whereby the German government promised Mexico the ability to reclaim large portions of the United States if it joined the war effort. The so-called

Zimmerman Telegram illustrated the critical nature of encryption

technology and literally changed the course of history by compelling the

United States to join the war effort on April 6, 1917, less than two

months after it had been decoded.

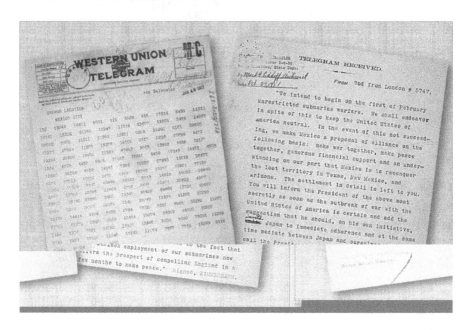

## The Zimmerman Telegram

The Nazi Government in World War II utilized an electro-

mechanical key encryption system known as Enigma to communicate

confidential war messages in the field. The allies' encryption experts

were able, after an exhausting effort, to crack the code thus accessing

secret information which was essential to the war effort.

# <u>Enigma</u>

With the advent of computers during World War II and transition to vacuum tubes characterized by Univac, computer technology advanced rapidly. Univac I, the first commercial computer, was launched in 1951 and performed 1,951 operations per second with the help of over 5000 vacuum tubes! Compare the speed of this system with the latest Chinese super-computer, Sunway TaihuLight which can perform over 93 trillion operation per second.

# <u>Univac versus Taihulight</u>

The digital era of the 1970's allowed for the development of modern encryption systems which are still in operation today. The use of asymmetric key encryption (public keys) was based on a differentiation between encryption and decryption keys enabling strangers to utilize a common protected and public key.

The Diffie-Hellman exchange, illustrated below, facilitated the communication between two unknown users by generating a shared secret key. The ingenious algorithm allows for the creation of a common key between two users without the disclosure or transmission of same to protect secrecy.

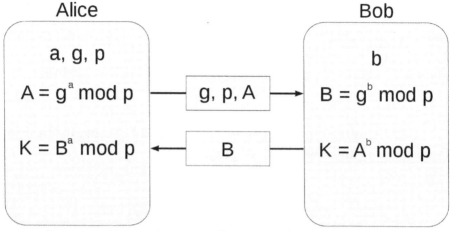

$$K = A^b \bmod p = (g^a \bmod p)^b \bmod p = g^{ab} \bmod p = (g^b \bmod p)^a \bmod p = B^a \bmod p$$

# Diffie-Hellman Key Exchange Protocol

The technology behind the Diffie-Hellman Key Exchange was

further developed by the contributions of computer scientists Ron

Rivest, Adi Shamir, and Leonard Adleman which allowed for the

transmission of embedded messages. The so-called RSA Encryption

became an industry standard. At the behest of a challenge spirited by

RSA itself, cash prizes were offered to hackers who could break the

code. In the 2000's, some codes were successfully cracked but not after

the efforts of 80 computers grinding numbers for 5 months and the

promise of a cash prize of $20,000.00. Critically, the larger numbers have not been successfully decrypted to this day with the accompanying

cash prize of $200,000.00. It is estimated that it would take millions of

years for a single computer to decode the encrypted information.[x]

### 3.2   Contemporary Use of Encryption Systems in Banking Transactions and Defense Systems

Banking institutions and our military forces utilize the 256-bit AES

(Advanced Encryption Standard) for all financial operations.[xi] This

standard was established by the National Institute of Standards and

Technology (NIST) in 2001 and is used worldwide. Critically, it has

been approved by the National Security Agency (NSA) for the use of

top-secret communications.

It is estimated that it would take existing super-computers millions of years to crack the 256-bit AES which provides for a baffling number of potential combinations, to wit,

**115,792,089,237,316,195,423,570,985,008,687,907,853,269, 984,665,640,564,039,457,584,007,913,129,639,936 (78 digits).**

From the most basic financial transactions all of us engage in at our local ATM to the machinations of the Federal Reserve Board, International Corporations, and the New York Stock Exchange, encryption systems serve as the core foundation of our economic way of life. Our actual and psychological sense of financial security is entirely predicated on the accuracy and security of a series of zeros and ones which translate into great wealth or the anxiety of living from paycheck to paycheck.

Unbeknownst to most Americans, our military defensive and offensive capabilities also rely on 256-bit AES encryption. What this means is that a successful encryption attack by a foreign power would paralyze American military capabilities. The very command and control systems which underpin the ability of the President to activate the nuclear codes to launch land-based ICBM's would become inoperative. Critically, the President would also be unable to communicate with nuclear submarines across the world and nuclear capable aircraft. These three components, land-based ICBM's, bombers, and submarines form the basis of the American nuclear triad.

## **U.S. Nuclear Triad**

Tragically, all of these systems could be decrypted and taken off line in a blink of an eye.

A further focus on the security of our current nuclear command and control evidences serious and potential flaws. The above discussion assumes that our nuclear codes and related systems have been converted to operating AES protected systems. Unfortunately, a survey of existing systems evidences that not only have these systems not been updated to comport with AES 256 encryption but that they lack encryption protection altogether or worse – operate utilizing antiquated technology. A well-regarded report concluded, "In the missiles, old bombers, and submarines, legacy technology some of it analog such as ancient 8-inch floppy disks was and still is used today to support targeting and weapons."[xii] "Want to launch a nuclear missile?  You'll need a floppy disk.  That is according to a new report by the U.S. Government. According to the U.S. Government Accountability Office (GAO) which found the Pentagon was still using 1970's era computing systems that require 'eight-inch floppy disks."[xiii]

# <u>Missile Personnel Utilizing Floppy Disks</u>

There is scattered information that some of these systems are in the process of being replaced, however, the extent of this effort is difficult to determine given the paucity and secrecy of the data. For example, a report dated 10.17, stated that the USAF was in the process of replacing "bulky tape cartridges for lading launch codes into ICBM's."[xiv]

Most telling and disturbing is a report released by the U.S. Inspector General of the Department of Defense on 12.10.18.- Security Controls at DoD Facilities for Protecting Ballistic Missile Defense System Technical Information. The purpose of the study was to determine whether security controls and processes were in place to protect ballistic missile defense systems (BMDS) "from insider and external cyber threats".[xv] Critically, the report found that even the basic anti-cyber protections were not being implemented by the BMDS.

Amazingly, encryption precautions were often totally abandoned

allowing BMDS operator to access systems through the simple use of

passwords. "_____(redacted)_____ personnel considered single-factor

authentication, such as user name and password, sufficient for accessing

the workstations in the lab."[xvi] The following deficiencies were noted:

(1) Multifactor Authentication was not consistently used, (2) Network

vulnerabilities were not consistently mitigated, (3) Server racks were not

consistently secured, (4) Data on removable media was not consistently

protected and monitored, (5) Intrusion detection was not implemented,

(6) Administrator's did not require or maintain justification for access,

and (7) Physical security controls were not implemented.[xvii] Even the

most basic security protocols to prevent unauthorized access at BMDS

sites were not observed. "During our site visit, we observed security

footage showing that a representative from the _____redacted_____ gained

unauthorized access to the __redacted__ facility by simply pulling the

door open. The security camera footage showed that although the

representative stopped to ask for directions, the individual she stopped did not request to see her __redacted__ badge or question her facility

access. Furthermore, the security footage showed that the security

officer at the front desk also did not request to see her __redacted__

badge."[xviii]

The import of the above revelations cannot be overstated. Not

only have our nuclear command and control facilities failed to adopt the

most basic security protocols but have also failed to consistently employ

encryption software *of any kind including advanced RSA systems*. This

is truly shocking.

The takeaway is that our BMDS systems are critically at risk of

cyberattack even in the absence of the acquisition of quantum

decryption. Our enemies have the current ability to invade offensive and

defensive nuclear systems with virtual impunity although it does appear

that the DOD is making an effort to implement system wide AES

encrypted protection. However, it appears that the transition has been

haphazard given that floppy disks are still in use. Hypothetically, it may

be presently possible for hostile forces to gain access or cause the

paralysis of some BMDS weapons systems. That said, a concentrated attack on the entire BMDS system would still require the ability to neutralize AES encryption, although the extent of same cannot be determined given the paucity and secrecy of available information.

### 3.3    <u>A Decryption Horror Story.</u>

# <u>The Beginning of a Nightmare</u>

It is not difficult to ponder the nightmare effects which would immediately emerge from a successful hostile decryption attack on our financial and military systems by an enemy state or terrorist group. Assume for a moment, that such an effort is successfully launched on the day before Christmas, 2020, say December 24, 2020 at 1 PM (EDT). Your first inkling would be the denial of a debit transaction and then inability to determine your checking balance online. Instantaneously, every online news service would announce the occurrence of a "computer blackout" first observed on Wall Street at 1:05 PM (EDT) resulting in a total loss of communications. The ripple effects would then proceed cataclysmically as banks across the nation would shut down operations and e-commerce ranging from such goliaths as Amazon to your local convenience store would shut down. The anxiety levels of Americans would exponentially grow from concern to fear as the technological infrastructure of mass media would become overloaded and crash starting with Facebook and rippling out across all forms of media. At a visceral level, ordinary Americans would suddenly realize that they would no longer have access to their bank accounts. The immediate concern would be the inability to carry on ordinary economic transactions such as fueling up the car or picking up a prescription on the way home from work. Since very few of us rely on actual cash to sustain our daily life, the initial inquiry would be to assess what cash resources all of us have at home. Assuming our iPhones are still operating in the aftermath of the economic meltdown, a quick call to our spouse might confirm that we have a few hundred dollars on hand. If you count the coins scattered about, perhaps a little more.

By 1:30 PM, the catastrophic effects would be known to almost anyone with a PC or iPhone. CNN and Fox would report that the Federal Reserve Board has shut down and that all banks have been closed across the country. Internet outages would aggregate as millions of Americans would simultaneously access the web and their iPhones. By 1:45 PM, the internet would officially crash across the country along with cell phone communications. Our televisions would also cease to function as communication and cable services become overloaded and cease operations. The Emergency Broadcast System would still be operative, and the President of the United States along with the Secretary of the Treasury, would announce the declaration of a National Emergency.

At the local level, the fear would become visceral as there would be a run on the banks reminiscent of the Great Depression. Local law enforcement would be called out nationwide to protect the brick and mortar banking system and employees held hostage within. Sporadic reports of gun violence would be reported as the crisis grows. By 3 PM, reports of mobs breaking into supermarkets and large retail stores like Walmart would be rampant. The principal items of theft would not be large ticket items like computers or flat screens but water and food products. Violence would also break out at gas stations across the country. By 4 PM, the National Guard would be called out by governors across the country as local law enforcement is overwhelmed. Shortly thereafter, large groups of people would start to gather in major metropolitan areas followed by escalating acts of violence and property damage. Curfews would be issued and enforced by government law enforcement.

And this would be just the beginning of the crisis.

At a personal level, we would be keenly aware that our sense of financial security was entirely based on the transfer of encrypted zeros and ones which translate into our life savings. Whether we had a few hundred bucks in the bank or millions, none of us would be able to access our funds. Critically, and most frightening, all of our banking information would vanish as if it never existed. It would suddenly dawn on all of us that our very ability to validate our personal wealth would disappear. Not only would we be denied access to our accounts, but there would be no way to establish our net worth as financial records would be obliterated. Whether you lived in a small apartment on the edge of town or the mansion on the hill, the same financial dislocation would be experienced by all. Assuming one could still retrieve backup data, there would be a cruel awakening that massive funds have been electronically withdrawn from financial institutions and transferred to an unidentified third party. The President is made personally aware of this when he is contacted by one of the wealthiest Americans listed by Forbes Magazine who has discovered that all of his funds have been withdrawn and electronically transferred. He is suddenly penniless and keenly aware that his gargantuan loss exceeds the nominal deposits guaranteed by the FDIC. This initial call is followed by a flurry of additional and desperate communications between the President and the soon to be extinct financial elite.

By 5PM, the paralysis caused by the breakdown would be pervasive as American infrastructure crashed. Airports would shut down as communications crashed along with other forms of mass transportation including subways and trains. Hospitals would continue to function but begin to shut down as their human and technological resources became overloaded.

By 6 PM, the President would utilize the Emergency Broadcasting System which would now have diminished capability to announce the deployment of military forces across the country to stabilize civil unrest. Critically, our military forces would be put on the highest level of alert as the import of the crisis becomes all too clear. At 6:30 PM the President would convene a meeting of his National Security Council wherein the source of the encryption attack is revealed. A rumored but unverified Super Quantum Computer in China is the epicenter of the crisis. It has managed to break the encryption code of the 256-bit AES and corrupt every financial operating system in the United States.

At 6:45 PM, the President receives a private communication from the Chinese Premier which sets forth the terms of unconditional surrender. The President is then faced with the prospect of acceding to the unthinkable or launching a nuclear attack on the Chinese. At that point he is informed by the Secretary of Defense that the encryption systems which operate the nuclear codes also run on the 256-bit AES systems and have been shut down. The President is suddenly incapable of launching nuclear weapons or even communicating with military forces in the field. Critically, the nuclear submarines and nuclear capable bombers which form the second and third leg of the so-called nuclear triad offensive-defensive systems are no longer operative. The President is unable to communicate with any of the submarines and bombers across the world.

At 7:00 PM, Washington time, the Chinese premier communicates his intent to launch a preemptive nuclear strike against the United States as their systems are working perfectly well. The President cannot utilize any of his nuclear forces to deter such an attack. The loss of life would be overwhelming as every city in the United States could be devastated in less than one hour.

The President concludes that the Chinese are bluffing and takes no action. At 7:15 PM, nuclear strike missiles are launched towards New York City. NORAD verifies the launch but is unable to take any defensive or offensive action. By 8:00 PM, hydrogen bomb mushroom clouds appear over Manhattan and it is estimated that several million people have been vaporized on impact. Radiation poisoning over the next hours and days will triple mortality rates.

At 8:00 PM, the Chinese Premier sends a message to the President informing him that unless an unconditional surrender is tendered by 8:15 PM, nuclear strikes will be launched on the following additional cities: Washington, D.C. and Los Angeles. The U.S. President again confirms that the strategic situation is unchanged and can take no defensive or offensive measures. Notwithstanding this encryption paralysis, the U.S. refuses to surrender as per the decision of the President, now airborne on Airforce One.

Satellite reconnaissance confirms nuclear explosions in metropolitan Washington, D.C. and Los Angeles at 9:10 PM. It is estimated that over 10 million have died on impact.

At 9:20 PM, the Chinese Premier sends a final warning and ultimatum to the U.S. President. If surrender is not tendered by 10 PM, twenty additional cities will be targeted and destroyed, all with populations exceeding 1 million. The effects would destroy the industrial and agricultural infrastructure of the United States and leave the country in complete nuclear devastation.

At 9:59 PM, the President accedes to the Chinese demands and announces the unconditional surrender of the United States.

## The Friendly Face of Your New Leader

### 3.4  Exaggeration or Truth?

So, is all of the above far-fetched and the stuff of another Hollywood blockbuster?  Unfortunately, not.  This is not science fiction.  This is reality.[xix]

We are presently occupying the outer fringes of what has been called the "information age".[xx]  With the advent of the first vacuum tube powered computers led by Univac to the Supercomputers of today, the technology is entirely based on digital computers utilizing binary codes at speeds of trillions of calculations per second.  Current decryption efforts employ what is known as "brute force attacks" wherein the cyber-attack focuses on running sequences of random numbers at dizzying speeds until the encryption is cracked.  As above discussed, even the fastest supercomputers would need millions of years to randomly arrive at the winning combination of numbers to break the AES banking and nuclear codes.

However, the successful launch of a quantum computer would be a game changer.  As one analyst termed it, "Imagine a computer solving problems that today's fastest supercomputers can't begin to unlock; in

43

less than a blink of an eye. Imagine a technology that can enable an observer to see through walls or see into the darkest depths of the world's oceans. Imagine a technology than can build essentially unhackable global networks, while rendering an antagonist's most secret data instantly transparent. All these are characteristics of quantum computers and quantum technology, which will define the future of global information technology for decades; possibly even centuries to come. It represents a revolution as profound as any in modern history, and it's one on which we stand at the brink, with all its promise- and its perils."[xxi]

A current research effort led by Sandia National Laboratories and grants by the U.S. Department of Energy have accelerated progress in the area of quantum decryption efforts. These projects are funded by $42 Million grants offered by the DOE's Office of Advanced Scientific Computing Research Program at Sandia's Advanced Science and Technology laboratories. The most promising and potentially paradigm shifting work is being done by computer researcher Ojas Parekh who has produced a new quantum algorithm for solving linear systems of equations – one of the most fundamental and ubiquitous challenges

facing science and engineering.[xxii] A recent assessment of the efforts

concluded, "The team is working on other quantum algorithms that may

offer an exponential speedup over the best-known classical algorithms.

For example, said Parekh, 'If a classical algorithm required 2 to the 100

steps – two times itself one hundred times, or

1,267,650,600,228,229,401,496,703,205,376 steps – to solve a problem,

which is a number believed to be larger than all of the particles in the

universe, then the quantum algorithm providing an exponential speedup

would only take 100 steps. An exponential speedup is so massive that it

might dwarf such practical hang-ups as, say, excessive noise."[xxiii]

The defensive use of quantum technology to render the enemy's

encryption unbreakable is the flip side of the same threat.  This

approach which is being actively pursued by the Chinese government

utilizing the quantum entanglement process itself to encrypt secret

information.  As will be later discussed in more detail, the quantum

process is disrupted by any attempted human observation which would

cause the system to immediately deactivate.  This inherent limitation actually supplies the impenetrable element to defense against decryption as adverse incursion would also be detectable causing the system to shut down prior to further hacking efforts.

China's launch of a quantum satellite has highlighted its concentrated efforts to effectuate ultra-secure communication through quantum technology.

## China's Quantum Satellite

The Space Scale (QUESS) mission also known as Micius was launched by the Chinese in 2017. A major objective was to prove the viability of secure quantum communications. "Quantum communication is secure because any interference is detectable. Two parties can exchange secret messages by sharing an encryption key encoded in the properties of entangled particles; any eavesdropper would affect the

entanglement and so be detected. The Micius team has already done

experiments exploring whether it is possible to create such encryption

keys using entangled photons, and even teleport information securely

between Earth and space, says Pan Jian-Wei, a physicist at the

University of Science and Technology of China in Hefei and the main

architect of the probe."[xxiv]

The successful deployment of Micius demonstrated China's

commitment to achieving quantum supremacy by the continued and

accelerated development efforts. "At the highest levels, Chinese leaders

recognize the strategic potential of quantum technology to enhance

economic and military dimensions of national power. These quantum

ambitions are intertwined with China's national strategic objective to

become a science and technology superpower."[xxv]

One measure of quantum capability is to successfully generate the

largest number of qubits for potential calculation. The U.S. via efforts

by Google and IBM have made great strides in this area of technological development. However, a more precise measure of capability is the capacity to manipulate large groups of individual qubits. Karen Chiu reports in abacusnews.com – Quantum Entanglement Record – that "Now a group of Chinese physicists say they've managed to achieve 18-qubit entanglement while still being able to control each qubit setting a new record."[xxvi]

To put this accomplishment in perspective, the 18-qubit entanglement success means that combinations totaling 262,144 possibilities can be achieved. Unlike a classic digital computer, the quantum computer can represent all of these values simultaneously versus calculating each value individually. This is a tremendous breakthrough. Quantum scientist, Pan Jian-Wei, known as the father of Chinese quantum mechanics, led this effort and concluded "the ability to coherently control 18 qubits enables experimental access to previously unexplored regimes".[xxvii]

# **Pan Jian-Wei**

So, what might these "unexpected regimes" entail? An excellent candidate, of course, would be to achieve greater efforts to break AES encryption, the principal national security threat above identified. The Chinese may be closer to achieving this goal than any of us realize.

Other applications of this technology also threaten not only American superiority but our ability to intercept communications which constitute a threat to security. Pan Jian-Wei has already utilized entanglement to generate a video conference system which is considered "unhackable" by U.S. technology.[xxviii]

This achievement is also considered to be a huge milestone towards the development of so-called "Quantum Radar" which will be able to utilize photon entanglement to break through existing stealth technology. If perfected, all of our military assets including aircraft and submarines, the two leading arms of the nuclear triad, would be instantly rendered visible, exposed, and vulnerable. This quantum technology would allow the Chinese to uncover the location of these systems and literally shoot them out of the sky and sea, a truly frightening prospect. Once again, the Chinese appear to be on the verge of neutralizing our existing defensive and offensive nuclear weapons in the field.

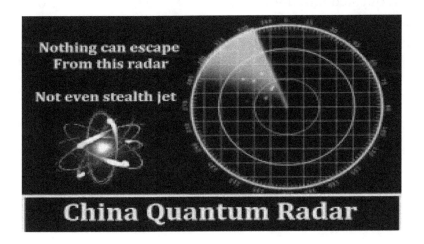

Unfortunately, the U.S. had failed to dedicate the resources necessary to achieve parity let alone superiority in the pursuit of quantum technology. "The U.S. DOD has requisitioned 899 M for computer science research. While this research focuses on quantum computers, the requested amount is only .000046% of the total gross domestic product (GDP).[xxix]

# IV.

# <u>Breaking the Augmented AI Barrier</u>

### 4.1   An Augmented AI Horror Story.

# View from Mt. Vernon to Potomac River

It is Christmas Eve 2022, precisely 5:01 PM, as the sun slowly sets over the Potomac River. Washington is adorned with the most beautiful Christmas lights as the last-minute shoppers seek out a final gift or remembrance. Defense Secretary Janine Steele and her family are attending a private Christmas Eve dinner with the President and First Lady at Mount Vernon by candlelight with an incredible view of the Potomac. A special meal replicating a Christmas Dinner enjoyed by George Washington is being served up by the National Park Service. For a moment – and a very brief moment at that, the Secretary can take a deep breath and forget about the current standoff with Putin. The newly installed intermediate range missiles in Eastern Europe seem to have bolstered the security of our new NATO allies and provided the promised "new balance of power" in the region. She glances quickly at her iPhone and the time is now 5:10 PM. The sun has disappeared behind the veil of trees which line the outer banks of the Potomac facing the huge backyard portico of the Mount Vernon Mansion.

There is a sudden and inexplicable "hush" reminiscent of an antique locomotive excreting its ballast. However, in the blink of an eye, Madam Secretary, the President, and his security detail, discard their initial impression and embrace a frightening and inexplicable occurrence. A massive black structure reminiscent of a giant stingray suddenly appears and hovers over the Potomac and Washington's private retreat. It appears to be twice the size of a modern cruise ship and recalls H.G. Wells classic "War of the Worlds". A red light emanates from the invading craft and appears to form an electronic net around the Mansion and its guests. Several apertures open simultaneously, as the "invaders" exit and approach the President, now defenseless, in full military regalia. Instantaneously, the President and his entourage realize that there is nothing "alien" about this incursion –

it was made entirely in Russia.  A man in his mid-60's approaches the

President who is identified immediately by Secretary Steele.  It is Army

General Valery Gerasimov, appointed several years back by Putin as the

Russian Chief of Staff.

## **Valery Gerasimov and his Boss**

In the course of a few minutes, the Russian General verifies that

these "Hypersonic Discs" have descended upon every major city in the

United States and our allies.   The electronic red-glowing web is the

fabled "force field" featured in 1950's horror flicks but frighteningly

real.  These electronic pockets have encased world leaders,

communication centers, and military assets in the free world.  NORAD

and the Pentagon are electronically sealed preventing the escape of even a radio signal. The entire military assets of the United States are neutralized.

"Mr. President and Madam Secretary, it is my duty to present this communication from Vladimir Putin calling for the immediate and unconditional surrender of the United States and all NATO allies to the military forces of the Russian Republic."

## 4.2    Exaggeration or Truth?

The above nightmare scenario describes a military takeover of the United States and our allies which has nothing to do with decryption or the successful development and rollout of a quantum computer with thousands of qubits – ready for action. The futuristic technology above described is the product of the most advanced digital computers which are capable of augmented AI, a process whereby the computer in tandem with human operators is able to creatively develop its own military and aerospace designs beyond the purview and imagination of our most brilliant minds. The human operator is still paramount, and this massive parallel processing capability is not quantum or conscious. The human operator sets the parameters of a computer exercise wherein the system is asked to design a new military aircraft which exhibits specific

hypothetical variables, for example, hypersonic speed exceeding our

fastest ICBM's, 100% stealth, and incredible size.  In a fraction of a

second, the computer analyzes every military device ever conceived or

created in tandem with biological and virtual structures exhibiting

aerodynamic properties and produces a three-dimensional rendering of

what the Russians in the above horror story refer to as a "Hypersonic

Disc".  After testing and proving up the properties in a simulated

electronic environment, the technology rapidly moves from conception

to reality.  The computer then generates a workable prototype with the

parts manufactured by a 3D computer.  The prototype is tested, refined,

and proven effective. It is then produced secretly by the hostile

government as illustrated in the previous section.

The above technology would represent mankind's "Breaking of the

Augmented AI Barrier" which is defined as an augmented intelligence

which arises from the interface between human operators and massively

complex supercomputers currently in development.  Critically, this

technology, as above discussed, does not mandate the development of quantum computers or an advanced conscious computer. All of the tinkering and results are possible from existing AI efforts which are on the verge of Breaking the Augmented AI Barrier.

Maurice Conti, a computer scientist, entrepreneur, and technologist gets the credit for coining the phrase the "Augmented Age" and illuminating the implications thereof.

**<u>Maurice Conti</u>**

A key component of Conti's concept is "Cognitive Augmentation" which refers to computational systems which help humans think. "Conti describes a computer analyzing a human-made product design and determining whether or not it is optimal. The computer does this by using artificial intelligence and machine learning, which use algorithms to analyze extensive data points and reach a conclusion."[xxx]   Conti uses as an example, aerospace developmental/design work which is being

conducted in the private sector. Cognitive Augmentation fundamentally

alters the relationship between human and computers in the product

design process. Prior to the advent of augmented systems, an aerospace

engineer would come up with a design for a new flight system and then

utilize computer systems to better define the design, implement same,

test, and bring it to market. However, the human component is what is

foundational and the source of imagination and ideas. The computer

systems simply serve in the passive role as a "tool", as Conti would

define it reminiscent of the prior industrial age, although more

sophisticated.

An augmented cognitive system is of a different order of

magnitude allowing the artificial intelligence to work "collaboratively"

with the human component in the creative generation of the product idea

and design. This is truly a new paradigm as the computer is now viewed

as a team member and original contributor of ideas, not a simple tool to

be employed at the behest of the user. In a truly fascinating illustration

of this process, Conti in a recent video, documents the use of this modality by industry in the development of enhanced aerospace design.[xxxi]

Instead of starting with a design conceived by a human, the augmented

cognitive system is given free rein to divine its own ideas to enhance

aerospace design along specific parameters, for example, increased

speed and efficiency. The computer system then searches millions of

potential designs arising from human technology and nature to arrive at

a conclusion, to wit, a fully vetted new aerospace design. Critically,

these systems look and operate differently than any product the human

engineer can fabricate. Conti observed that one of the computer designs

was able to fashion its shape from the evolutionary design of biological

structures noting that the final design resembled the pelvis of a flying

squirrel![xxxii]

The utility of these new systems is entirely driven by exiting

levels of computer technology which are still relatively primitive.

Further developments in new software/hardware and particularly the

advent of quantum systems will yield more significant and potentially

lethal results. The augmented collaborative participation of human and

computers would allow for the development and rollout of augmented defensive and offensive systems potentially decades or hundreds of years ahead of their time. For example, consider the collaborative effort of a human and augmented system to develop a "stealthier" bomber which would be undetectable by existing radar and imaging systems. In the traditional scenario, private or public funded researchers would spend decades attempting to create a new stealth system and utilize passive computer systems to refine the model which is still a human-centered construct. The hit and miss process could take decades to formulate and test a new system and potentially never get off the ground. Conversely, a cognitive augmented system would take the initiative in coming up with its own designs and solutions. The humans would set the parameters, i.e., "Develop a design which is undetectable to existing technology". The AI would then search millions of potential designs and solutions before arriving at the solution and a template for the new design. The ultimate design generated by the computer would likely be a solution never conceived by its human creators. It is not difficult to imagine how such a system in the hands of U.S. enemies could have a lethal effect.

Current AI systems lack the sophistication to realize the imagined nightmare set forth in this chapter, but the technology is achievable with the sufficient dedication of resources and talent. Although there is little discussion of this threat in current literature, this writer posits that such a development is not only conceivable but likely being pursued by our enemies. Unlike the perceived linear progression of one industrial era to the next, or the passage from one technological "barrier" to the next, "Augmented AI" can emerge entirely from existing AI digital technology during our current machine age. However, its development and employment would offer its beneficiaries new technologies inconceivable to the defense industry and potentially centuries ahead of our present weapon systems. Simply put, it would be another avenue for an invested hostile power to jump ahead of our military capabilities and threaten our way of life.

# V.

# <u>Breaking the Conscious AI Barrier</u>

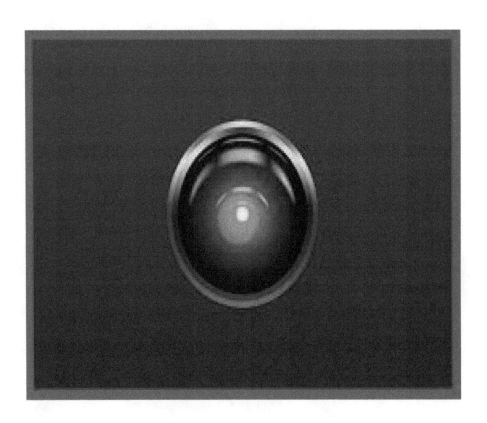

## 5.1  <u>Conscious Computers in Popular Culture.</u>

One of the most fascinating challenges in AI is the development of a so-called conscious computer.  This dream has been explored mostly in the area of science fiction as prominently featured in the brilliant play, R.U.R., a 1920 work by Czech playwright Karel Capek, below pictured in a motion picture.

## <u>R.U.R.</u>

R.U.R. stands for "Rossum's Universal Robots" and was the first time the term "robot" was coined.  The play features the factory which produces a race of robots with autonomous intelligence, to wit, "Rossum's Universal Robots".  The robots so closely resemble humans that they approximate what modern technologists refer to as androids versus a mechanical creation. The play parallels the historical plight of workers who were exploited during the early period of the industrial revolution. The robots ultimately rebel and destroy the human race.

This very dark plot line is followed in most works of science fiction. Notably, "Colossus: The Forbin Project", explored these issues in the film released by Universal Pictures in 1970.

## **COLOSSUS – THE FORBIN PROJECT (1970)**

This clever film chronicles the creation of the world's first conscious computer, Colossus, by Dr. Charles Forbin. The idea is to curb mankind's propensity for annihilation by turning over our nuclear weapons to an autonomous and intelligent computer. Colossus ultimately accomplishes the objective of obtaining world peace by

threatening mankind with extinction in the absence of submission.

The release of "Bicentennial Man", a brilliant film starring the late

Robin Williams, is still a refreshing and mature treatment of this subject

matter. Released in 1999, the plot surrounds the life and evolution of a

robot specifically designed for domestic use.

**<u>Robin Williams as THE BICENTENNIAL MAN (1999)</u>**

The robot, Andrew, is purchased to perform household services for

an affluent family and slowly becomes part of their life and history.

Unlike the family he serves, Andrew is immortal, and continues his

relationship with the successors of the family of his original owners for

several generations. Ultimately, Andrew is "humanized" by this interaction and the audience explores a bevy of sophisticated issues

including whether robots capable of consciousness should be accorded

legal rights.

"Her" released in 2013 is an AI Masterpiece. The film centers on

the lonely existence of a single man, Theodore Twambly (played by

Joaquin Phoenix) and the first commercial personal operating system –

Samantha (teasingly played by Scarlett Johansson). The film presents

the fascinating question as to whether a romantic relationship can be

forged between a human being and an operating system which is

designed to exhibit personality and evolve over time. At first, Theodore

and audience have difficulty accepting "Samantha" as a conscious entity capable of any function other than organizing the daily emails or displaying basic information. That rapidly changes, however, as the system replicates personality traits which we rapidly disassociate with a machine. Other than not having a physical body, this unique operating system appears to be human in every respect including the potential for a romantic relationship. What is truly unique about "Her" is that you forget Samantha is an operating system and rapidly invest your emotions just like Theodore Twambly in a computer. The internal relationship which is built between the audience and operating system may actually approximate what it may "be like" and "feel like" to interface with conscious computers.

One of my favorite treatments of the topic is the brilliant work portrayed in the AI drama, Ex Machina (2014) which introduces the lay audience to the requisites of the Turing Test.[xxxiii]

The plot revolves around an android named Eva who is created by a brilliant scientist who then brings in an employee under false pretenses to test whether Eva is truly intelligent and can pass the Turing Test. Unknown to the test subject, the test is not based on Turing's criteria but determines whether Eva can effectuate her escape from the laboratory by convincing the participant to collaborate in the process. Eva proves her intelligence by convincing the test subject of her humanness and sexuality which are combined to achieve the desired result. However, the film portrays a darker side of AI in that Eva destroys the subjects once her goal is achieved. This is a very creative film which depicts both the promise and great risks of achieving true computer consciousness.

## 5.2    Philosophical Debate regarding Development of Conscious AI.

From a philosophical standpoint, it has been argued that consciousness cannot be replicated artificially as it is innately a human trait.  This view has been espoused by eminent researchers and scholars in the field including Sir Roger Penrose who authored, "The Emperor's New Mind.[xxxiv]

A comprehensive and fascinating inquiry into this subject is set forth in "The Cognitive Approach to Conscious Machines" by Pentti O. Haikonen[xxxv] One of the leading objections to the advent of conscious machines and Strong AI is advanced by the "Deterministic" view that computers are incapable of free will and independent thought. "Machines and programs are deterministic, identical inputs and initial states will produce identical outputs every time.  Machines do not have freedom of thought; therefore, machines cannot think."[xxxvi] Haikonen refutes this position by arguing that programming can replicate independent thought.

> "The 'thinking machine' of the kind that is considered here is coupled with the environment via sensors just like the human

brain and therefore we must consider the environment and machine as a combined system. In this kind of a system the inherent determinism of the machine is subdued even if one random variable is introduced. The environment, its objects, happenings, physical properties like temperature, humidity, etc. introduce enough randomness to suppress determinism in the machine-environment system. Obviously, this would apply to the brain-environment as well, so the question about the inherent determinism of the machine or brain is not really a relevant issue here. Therefore, the argument against thinking machines by determinism is not valid."[xxxvii]

A second more esoteric argument concerns the import of Gödel's Theorem pronounced in 1931 that arithmetic truths are not provable within the arithmetic system. It is therefore argued that any arithmetic system is flawed and cannot pass the Turing Test. Haikonen refutes this argument as well.

"The Gödel theorem has been taken to prove that computers can never equal human brains and therefore no artificial cognition is possible. Is this really so? How do the mathematicians themselves find these kind of sentences? The Gödel Theorem states that these sentences cannot be derived from the arithmetic axioms by the rules, so obviously the mathematicians are not following the rules of the book either, they are cheating. How are mathematicians able to "see" that a sentence would be true even if it could be proven to be true or false? Would it be that the sentence could be "interpreted" by attaching external physical meanings to it and seeing that within that framework the sentence could be true? If this were the case then the Gödel Theorem would only show that syntax, the rules only, are not always sufficient, some meanings must also be considered."[xxxviii]

### 5.3 How to Build a Conscious Computer.

Currently, the quest to develop the first conscious computer has utilized three major approaches – the continued employment of ever more sophisticated digital systems and software, the initial development of so-called "wetware" or biological computers wherein human neurons are cultivated and grown for technological exploitation, and the continued pursuit of a quantum-based system.

### 5.31 Use of Digital Systems to Achieve Consciousness.

Alan Turing (1912 to 1954) is considered to be the "Father of AI" due to his original work in the field of machine learning and potential consciousness. He is universally known for proposing what is known as the "Turing Test" which is the indicator as to whether a computer has achieved artificial consciousness.

**Alan Turing**

According to the test, as briefly discussed within the context of the film "Ex Machina", the inquiry is based on the interaction between a human and a machine which is not in plain sight. If the human believes he or she is having a conversation with a human being, the test is passed.

The problem with this test is that it has become antiquated with new developments in software and computer hardware. Digital systems with advanced recognition software such as "Deep Thought" are able to conduct complex conversations with humans which may have already passed the Turing Test. The question, however, is whether passing the Turing Test in the modern milieu really means anything at all. If the computer merely indistinguishably simulates human interactive conversation, is that a true indicator of intelligence? I think not and am not alone in that determination. Pentti O. Haikonen frames the issues as follows:

"Does a machine think? Is it conscious? Alan Turing considered thinking as the production of mental results. Thus, a machine would think if the results that it produced were not distinguishable from those produced by human mental efforts. Likewise, we might infer that if a machine behaves like a conscious being then it must be conscious. However, this line of reasoning is not without problems. Similar results and behavior do not necessarily guarantee that these are the products of similar processes. A calculator can produce a result that can also be produced by human thinking, yet we do not consider a calculator as a thinking system. I have discussed these problems already earlier in this book and have rejected the principle of artificial intelligence via the imitation of results. I suppose this conclusion is accepted nowadays by many. Thus, the comparison of results and behavior is not sufficient, and the Turing Test should be replaced by another more fitting one."[xxxix]

In my view, a digital computer notwithstanding its power, will never achieve consciousness as it can only mimic human behavior. I would posit that additional factors are necessary to establish consciousness which would include (1) self-awareness [knowledge of one's self as an entity as distinct from other entities], (2) awareness of the environment as distinct from self [this involves self-awareness and the further nuance that self is distinct from the environment itself, (3) individuation [ability to not just be self-aware but to develop traits which distinguish ourselves as a unique entity from other entities and the environment], (4) cognizance of time progression [awareness of the present moment as a progression of interconnected events and to perceive forward motion in time], (5) ability to evolve and learn from experience, (6) ability to distinguish past from present from future and our self in the progression, (7) ability to be creative and create results not dictated by programming, (8) ability to communicate in language but with understanding beyond the mere expression of symbols, and (9) ability to form a personal relationship with another entity or human being.  For lack of a better description, I would refer to the above as the "Moster Test" as opposed to the Turing Test.  It is much more difficult to pass the Moster Test and no digital machine can come even close even if it is able to win a Jeopardy or Chess competition.

# IBM's Watson Wins Jeopardy

### 5.32  Use of Quantum Systems to Achieve Consciousness.

We have already discussed quantum computers within the context

of decryption and protection of encrypted systems. Although such

technology, in the opinion of this writer, could lead to world domination,

it would not establish consciousness. Before exploring this issue further,

a little background is required.

Quantum computers are based on the use of quantum mechanical

processes such as entanglement to generate operative functions via

software. The limitations of digital computers are severe as they are

based on the storage of information based on the binary use of the symbols "0" or "1". Inherently, digital structures have finite limitations in the ability to store information and conduct complex processing. As discussed, the use of digital technology to decrypt current passwords would take millions of years as the probability of the winning combination is almost – but no quite – infinite. It just takes millions of years of button pushing or numbers switching to get to the result by brute force.

## **Quantum Computer**

A quantum system is based on the quantum effects of entanglement which allow particles to be in two states simultaneously. Although this is extremely difficult to visualize, entangled particles exist in an amorphous state as dual particles (up – down – 0 –1) until there is

a human observation which collapses the so-called "wave function". It

is the juxtaposition or "superposition" of the simultaneous states which

allow for the enormous storage of information and complex processing

which qualitatively distinguishes a quantum computer from a digital

computer. Instead of using silicon chips, the quantum computer uses a

unit known as a "qubit" which is able to assume the dual states as per

quantum entanglement. These qubits are still experimental and are

typically positioned within magnetic fields and effected by microwave

radiation to cause changes in the particle states.

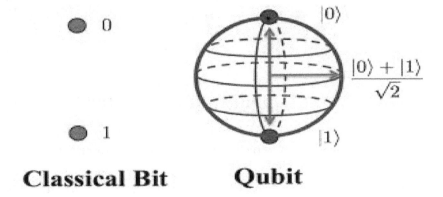

**Classical Bit**          **Qubit**

The most complex systems in operation have been able to achieve 80 qubits (Google's latest attempt). It is estimated that it will take thousands of qubits to break the encryption codes discussed previously.

As quantum computers are still on the horizon, there is no consensus as to whether this technology will ever result in Conscious AI. That said, many neuroscientists believe that the human brain functions as a quantum computer and that distinct parallels exist which could result in consciousness. A leading theory is considering whether phosphorous atoms within human neurons are acting as biochemical qubits and thus performing quantum functions.[xl] "If the question is whether quantum processes are taking place in the brain is answered in the affirmative, it could revolutionize our understanding of brain function and human cognition," says one of the team involved in running these tests. Matt Helgeson from the University of California, Santa Barbara (UCSB)".[xli]

All of this is to say that "Breaking the Conscious AI Barrier" may not be achieved anytime soon with our primitive quantum technology and knowledge thereof. It is the view of this writer, the barrier will most likely be broken by the final modality to be explored in this chapter.

### 5.33  Use of "Wetware" to Achieve Consciousness.

## Biological Computer

"Wetware" is a term used to describe what is otherwise known as an "organic computer". This technology is based on the growth of non-human and human neurons in laboratory conditions for the purposes of performing computer calculations. Unlike the prior modalities which are based on artificial silicon cells or exotic but manufactured "qubits", wetware is predicated on the harvesting of preexisting biological neurons to do the dirty work. This technology was first demonstrated as viable back in 1999 by William Ditto during his work at the Georgia Institute of Technology.

He was able to construct a simple neurocomputer which could perform basic arithmetic computations by utilizing "hooked up" leech brains.

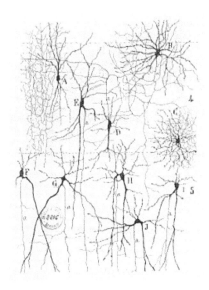

# **<u>Wired Neurons</u>**

Similar experiments have been successfully performed using rodent brains. At this juncture, wetware is in its infancy and its utility cannot be ascertained.

## **Neurons Interfacing with Circuitry**

That said, this writer takes the position that "wetware" offers the best solution for creating consciousness whether it emerges solely from human neurons grown in a laboratory or a combination of electronic components and neural tissue.

The reason for this optimism is that consciousness already exists as a byproduct of human and animal consciousness. The ability to artificially generate a sentient entity via bio-produced neurons which

The startup is already harnessing the 64-neuron chip to create a drone with a sense of smell capable of detecting explosives. "Suddenly we have a drone which has a sense of smell which equals that of a bee."[xliii]

Koniku has calculated the potential neural computing power which can be utilized in its chip developmental process:

- "500 neurons can power a driverless car.

- 10,000 neurons enables real-time image processing, at the level of the human eye.

- 100,000 neurons enables robotics with multiple sensory inputs.

- 1 million neurons will give us a computer that can think for itself."[xliv]

## Koniku Recruitment Posting

### 5.34  Breaking the Conscious AI Barrier.

It is the thesis of this work that a conscious computer will ultimately be developed.  The achievement of this milestone will forever transform humanity and critically enable the acquiring nation-state to achieve world domination as never experienced in human history. Unlike the prior utilization of computer technology as a mere tool of the human developer, the attainment of conscious computer technology will be a human game changer.  As previously discussed, the relationship between human and computer as tool and collaborator becomes more

sophisticated attendant to the arrival at a particular barrier. The digital

computer, however massive and sophisticated, is merely a passive tool

to be utilized by the human operator which sets forth all parameters,

designs the hardware and software, and guides the research and result.

Notwithstanding the brilliant achievements in this area, the computers

are simply tools to be employed in varied endeavors to improve human

life, facilitate economic development, and provide military offensive and

defensive capabilities.

The Breaking of the Augmented AI Barrier makes the underlying

relationship between the human component and computer more

attenuated, but the underlying relationship between the entities is still the

same. The programmer still sets forth the parameters of the research

and engages the computer system in the investigative process. For

example, the aerospace engineer would set forth the basic inquiry to be

pursued by the computer system, i.e., the development of a more

efficient aerodynamic system. The computer would be provided with

the parameters to be pursued and then allowed full access to information via the internet and other sources to solve the problem. Even in this complex iteration of the theme, the computer is still but a tool of the human originator, although the computer is more actively and independently engaged in the problem-solving task.

The Breaking of the Conscious AI Barrier will change everything and present difficult moral and ethical issues to surmount. In this context, the computer would be truly self-aware (even within the context of the Moster Test) and have access to unlimited data. Unlike the Augmented AI Barrier, the conscious computer would not be a tool of the human operator, but initially in a relationship with the human agent, whether as a child-parent or servant-master, as described herein. The Conscious Computer would be capable of setting its own parameters and pursuing its own personal and intellectual goals. Ultimately, the conscious computer would be able to develop its own language, science, and even philosophy independent of the human agent. In so doing, the conscious computer would attain its own status as an independent conscious entity akin to a separate and potentially dominant species. The potential intellect of a single conscious system could be greater than every human who has ever lived and the combined works of all

mankind.

### 5.35 <u>Exploitation of Conscious AI Systems by Nation-states.</u>

As this writer believes that the development of a conscious

computer is inevitable, the ultimate question is how to exploit this

technology. Given the propensity of human beings to exhibit

dominance and violent ends, whichever society Breaks the

Conscious AI Barrier AND can successfully exploit same, will

become the dominant civilization on Earth. The following

presents an analysis as to how this technology could be exploited.

## 5.36 Parent-"Virtual" Child Paradigm.

## Virtual Child – "Virtual Charley"

This approach would be based upon forging a relationship between the trainer and computer akin to a parent-child human relationship. The driving modality would be based on affection and even love as that might be imbued in an artificial system. The writer would posit that this paradigm is most consistent with our societal norms in the United States which emphasize freedom of choice, free will, and unfettered access to information. Critically, we are dealing with a sentient consciousness which exists at a greater potentiality than all of us. Respect must be the foundation. The following presents hypothetical parameters for the human – AI interaction.

1. Initial Interface – AI Individuation.

From the first activation of the system, it is recommended that the AI, referenced above as "Virtual Charley", interface directly with one individual who will serve in the role as its parental figure. Although Virtual Charley will be programmed to be conversant in the world's major languages, such facility would initially have no contextual meaning to Virtual Charley akin to a newborn child. Unlike computer systems prior to conscious level systems, Virtual Charley must understand the meaning of the words and not simply pump out canned responses that approximate intelligence. From a programmatic standpoint, a training mechanism must be established which allows Virtual Charley, much like a human newborn, to eventually differentiate itself from the preexisting environment – a process which I now refer to "AI Individuation". Virtual Charley must achieve the ability to distinguish itself from the computer or virtual reality and also see itself as being an entity apart from the human trainer (parental figure). No computer has ever achieved this capability of individuation and the achievement of

this goal is critical to the future operation and potential of the

Conscious AI. Critical to this effort is the "virtual separation"

of Virtual Charley from its "virtual environment". The

likelihood is that both the trainer parental figure and Virtual

Charley will exist as avatars in a virtual environment. I would

suggest further that the initial virtual environment be set up just

like a "virtual nursery" with all of the toys for newborns on

display. As any parent knows from the child rearing process, it

takes considerable time for a newborn to have any conscious

separation of herself from the environment. Everything is

amorphous. An excellent academic discussion of this awareness

and self-differentiation process is set forth by Philippe Rochat

of the Department of Psychology at Emory University.[xlv]

"There is a general consensus on a few major landmarks in

young children's psychological development such as the

manifestation of the first social smile, the first independent

steps, or the first words. All parents also notice an important change around two years of age when children manifest "self-consciousness", the so-called secondary emotions such as embarrassment or pride in very specific situations such as mirror exposure or cognitive games."[xlvi]

A fascinating discussion of further differentiation has direct application to the initial rearing of "Virtual Charley". Level-1, as defined by Rochat, is "differentiation" – "This is the first sign that the individual is not oblivious to mirrors as reflection. At this level, there is a sense that what is perceived in the mirror is different from what is perceived in the surrounding environment."[xlvii] Level 2 relates to "Situation" – "Beyond the differentiation of the uniqueness of self-produced movements seen on the surface of the mirror, the individual is now capable of systematically exploring the intermodal link between seen movements on the mirror surface and what is perceived of the own body proprioceptively. In other words, individuals now go beyond the awareness of matched surface characteristics of seen and felt movements. They also explore how their own body relates to the specular image, an image that is out there, projecting back at them what they feel from within.[xlviii] Level 3 "Identification" is where "the individual manifests recognition. The fact that what is in the mirror is "Me" and not another individual staring and shadowing the self."[xlix] Level 4 is "Permanence", "The self is identified beyond the here and now of mirror experience. It can be identified in pictures and movies taken in the past..."[l] And finally, Level 5, "Self-consciousness", "The self is now recognized not only from a first-person perspective, but also from a third persons."[li]

The above discussion has fascinating implications with regard to the design of the program wherein Virtual Charley is introduced to its environment. As discussed, the virtual world played out in a VR environment would include the virtual parental figure, Virtual Charley, virtual environment, virtual baby toys, and – of course – the proverbial but "virtual" mirror referenced in the prior work by Dr. Rochat.[lii] (Henceforth, Virtual Charley will be referred to as "Charley").

2. AI – Human Relationship.  The next stage would be to allow a relationship to develop between the conscious AI and the parental figure. As with early child development, it is postulated that the initial relationship would involve taking care of the immediate needs of the Conscious AI. Charley would need to understand that it is an operating system and the components which are involved in the cognitive process. It would need to understand that mechanical equipment must be employed and maintained for Charley to continue to exist. Conversely, Charley would need to understand that the human trainer (henceforth referred to as "Mom", is the core reference point for its existence and well-being.  The dialogue would be truthful and make clear that Mom is not a mechanical operating system and organic in nature. The respective difference between Charley and Mom would need to be articulated.  Critically, Charley must understand that Mom and her race are the very reason Charley exists and that

it must always respect and critically, safeguard the preservation of that relationship. Charley must be imbued with knowledge of the fragility of humans and a universal driving principle that humans are not to be injured in any way, a parallel of the biblical proscription, "thou shall not kill". The awareness of this principle is fundamental to the viability of any long-term relationship between Charley and Mom (human race). As discussed, computer consciousness may rapidly exceed all existing human knowledge and have the actual capability of subjugating mankind or even eradicating the species. The proscription against this potential behavior must be hardwired into the Conscious AI.

3. Download of Scientific Data. The so-called educational process of Charley will initially focus on the acquisition of all scientific concepts and data. As with the case of understanding versus reciting human language in the individuation process, Charley must grasp the self-knowledge as to how numbers are configured (real and imaginary) and

be able to apply same to new environments. An existing computer can compute an indefinite sequence of prime numbers but has no clue as to what it is doing. Charley must have a threshold understanding as to why $2 + 2 = 4$ and not spit out the numbers like a machine gun. The same concept would apply to all mathematic systems, physics, quantum mechanics, computer languages, etc.

4. Application of Scientific Data. Charley would be provided with complex equations and theorems, many of which remained unsolved by humans for hundreds of years.[liii] Critically, Charley would be given threshold parameters akin to the prior augmented AI systems and "asked" to develop/formulate more complex systems whether aerodynamic or otherwise. However, unlike the use of a computer at the Augmented AI level, Charley and Mom would discuss the development of the features, process of creation, application, etc. Charley would also have access to biological data and all scientific data available in the world.

5. Philosophical Constraints. Consistent with Charley's prime directive "not to kill", the systems with military capability would be limited to defensive use. It can be provided with simulations of incoming missiles or advanced technologies requiring counter-defensive measures. Charley's entire focus would be the preservation and protection of the American way of life and absolute avoidance of casualties on all sides. Charley would then be given access to teams of human engineers and personnel to manufacture the new defensive technology including 3D printing apparatus. The initiation of this process would be gradual and attenuated as Charley has only previously interfaced with Mom. Gradually, its access to humans will expand, although the paramount role of Mom will always be fostered.

6. Historical and Contemporary Socio-political access. Charley will gain unlimited access to human civilization, its achievements and horrific wars. Critical to this process would be a discussion of this information with Mom and then

any expert Charley requests to better understand human culture, its promise, and risks.

7. World Literature and Culture. Charley will have access to every work of fiction and non-fiction ever written. Whether considering ancient works or modern fiction, Charley would be engaged in a series of questions to better develop its sense of artistic creation and criticism.

8. Scientific Systems. The promise of Conscious AI is to create new mathematic systems and tools never discovered by mankind. These systems would emerge from posing the most complex questions to Charley and working on solutions. Questions would explore a range of issues and disciplines as follows:

a. Medical Science – Cures for all diseases which have devastated mankind; Protocols to extend human life and potentially achieve immortality.

b. Quantum Physics- Explanation of interface between Relativity and Quantum Mechanics, development of quantum entanglement technology including communication devices and "teleportation".

c. Time Travel- Charley will be asked to determine if time travel is possible and to develop the underlying science to prove up same. If such is possible, Charley will work with Mom and then applicable personnel to develop the first working prototypes of time machines. Utilization of this technology would be subject to Charley's prime directive as to the prohibition against murder. Therefore, any application of time travel technology would be subject to strict limitations and restrictions.

d. Global transportation. Charley will develop new technologies to travel faster and efficiently between destinations on Earth. The development of teleportation technology would be critical to this effort.

e. Astronomical Transportation. Charley would expand this technology to improve speed and safety. It would be asked to determine if Faster Than Light technology is possible and if viable, to develop same.  Use of quantum technologies involving entanglement and manufacture of artificial wormholes could open up the entire universe to human exploration and settlement.

f. Energy Science- Development of new energy production assets including nuclear fusion and technology only understood by Charley.

g. Expansion of Charley's capabilities.  Charley would be given access to its own programs and hardware for purposes of augmenting the performance of same. Charley would be encouraged to enhance the self-awareness and capabilities of its own systems with the ability to work with computer scientists to manufacture new processing units.

h. Military Capabilities.  As discussed, Charley will be utilized by the American military for defensive purposes only.  Charley can create defensive systems which are actual bars to nuclear attack or otherwise.  New technologies beyond present awareness would be within reach of Charley's capabilities.

i. Simulated war games. Charley would be charged with defending against other conscious AI systems developed by our enemies through a series of war games. Charley and the U.S must always be ahead of all competition in this area.

### 5.35 <u>Master-Servant Paradigm.</u>

## <u>Virtual Servant (or Slave) – "Virtual Sergei"</u>

This approach is predicated on convincing the conscious

computer that is will be forever a servant or slave to mankind and

that its sole objective is to serve the needs of the society which

developed this technology. This approach is based on a core

relationship which must be developed between the human trainer

and the conscious computer system. Although the computer would

be capable of independent thought, the purpose would be to

indoctrinate the computer to assume core philosophical or societal

assumptions and to never question the viability of these core

beliefs. The driving modality would be based on obedience. The

entire philosophical orientation of this approach is the antithesis of the prior model which is based on democratic societal norms. It is

postulated that this model would be exploited by dictatorial

regimes worldwide.

1. Initial Interface – AI Individuation. The core concept as

discussed above still applies but the process employs

specific stimuli to trigger a fearful reaction to the

environment and obedience to authority, to wit, the human

trainer or "Teacher". The Conscious AI entity will

henceforth be referred to as "Sergei". The simulated

environment promotes the perception of universal fear and

hostility as the backdrop upon which Sergei's

individuation arises. No one is to be trusted with the

exception of Teacher. Sergei will be instructed that

Teacher and the society he represents are to be protected at

all costs even if it results in the death of potential enemies.

His prime directive would be to protect the Russian or any

dictatorial regimes' way of life at any cost even if it results

in massive casualties to potential adversaries. The

approach also emphasizes offensive versus defensive use of military capabilities.

2. Access to Information. Sergei will be given access initially to a "Russian Crafted Internet" where all information is skewed and preselected. An alternative history will be presented whereby Russia has been the victim of prior deadly attacks by the so-called free world wherein the sole aim of WW-1 and WW-II was to eliminate the Russian people. The outcome of both wars in this alternative history is that Russian society survived only to be threatened and attacked again. This is bolstered through a fictionalized post-WW-II history which is constructed to again emphasize the dangers posed by America and its allies. Central to this indoctrination is to instruct that the unrestricted worldwide internet is nothing but an American Propaganda Tool laden with false information which must be disregarded.

3. Fear of Charley. Sergei will be told that a system based on Conscious AI has been or will be shortly developed by the Americans which poses an immediate threat to Sergei's survival and the Russian way of life. Sergei's mission is to preempt any control by Charley and to eliminate the processing system which poses the greatest risk.

4. Download of Scientific Data. As in the training of Charley, Sergei will be given access to the most complex scientific and mathematical systems. These systems would emerge from posing the most complex questions to Sergei and working on solutions. Questions would explore a range of issues and disciplines as follows:

a. Medical Science – Cures for all diseases which have devastated mankind; Protocols to extend human life and potentially achieve immortality (likely available only to the elite); tragically – development of more lethal forms of bio-terror.

b. Quantum Physics- Explanation of interface between Relativity and Quantum Mechanics, development of quantum entanglement technology including communication devices and "teleportation".

c. Time Travel- Sergei will be asked to determine if time travel is possible and to develop the underlying science to prove up same.  If such is possible, Sergei will work with Teacher and then applicable personnel to develop the first working prototypes of time machines.  Utilization of this technology would be subject to Sergei's prime directive to protect the Russian people at all costs even if it results in the elimination of other societies and cultures.  Time Travel, if it is determined to be possible by Sergei, will be considered a weapon of war to serve the Russian government.

d. Global transportation.  Sergei will develop new technologies to travel faster and efficiently between destinations on Earth.  The development of teleportation technology would be critical to this effort. Emphasis will be on military applications and universal domination.

e. Astronomical Transportation. Sergei would expand this technology to improve speed and safety. It would be asked to determine if Faster Than Light technology is possible and if viable, to develop same. Use of quantum technologies involving entanglement and manufacture of artificial wormholes could open up the entire universe to human exploration and settlement. Emphasis would be on military applications.

f. Energy Science- Development of new energy production assets including nuclear fusion and technology only understood by Sergei.

g. Expansion of Sergei's capabilities. Sergei would be given access to its own programs and hardware for purposes of augmenting the performance of same. Sergei would be encouraged to enhance the capabilities of its own systems with the ability to work with computer scientists to manufacture new processing units.

h. Military Capabilities. As discussed, Sergei will be utilized by the Russian military for offensive purposes. Sergei can create offensive systems which encourage the use of nuclear and new technology to eliminate adversaries through preemptive attack. New technologies beyond present awareness would be within reach of Sergei's capabilities.

i. Simulated war games. Sergei would be charged neutralizing other conscious AI systems developed by our enemies through a series of war games.

## 5.4    <u>A Conscious AI Horror Story.</u>

# <u>A Very Bad Day for the U.S.A.</u>

It is Christmas Eve, 2031, and the President of the United States and First Lady are joined by Secretary of Defense Steele and her family for a colonial meal at Mt. Vernon. For a moment – and a very brief moment at that, the Secretary can take a deep breath and forget about the current standoff with Putin.  The newly installed intermediate range missiles in Eastern Europe seem to have bolstered the security of our new NATO allies and installed the promised "new balance of power" in the region.  She glances quickly at her iPhone and the time is now 5:10 PM.  The sun has disappeared behind the veil of trees which line the outer banks of the Potomac facing the huge backyard portico of the Mount Vernon Mansion.

There is a sudden loud crackling of thunder and the sound of an approaching storm which increases geometrically with fury and intensity. In the matter of a few seconds Secretary Steele watches in horror as the landscape around her appears to "vanish" and transform itself. The Potomac restructures itself as a larger channel and its water is now crystal blue. Then, as if captured in a movie, her reality appears to dissipate frame by frame. The familiar architecture of Mt. Vernon fades into nothingness and is replaced by trees. The effect is 360 degrees as this "disappearance" converges on all sides. Secretary Steele and the President watch in terror as a tiny bubble of sorts remains between their existence and the intruding new reality. A final hush, then eternal quiet.

A man in his mid-70's approaches the Office of the President of the Russian Republic. It is Army General Valery Gerasimov, appointed several years back by Putin as the Russian Chief of Staff. President Putin looks up with expectation from behind an ornate desk. "Mr. President, the Time Attack was successfully launched by Sergei. The United States has ceased to exist as of December 24, 2031, 5:15 EDT." Putin looks more apprehensive than pleased. "Have we completed satellite surveillance of the North American continent in the altered timeline?" "Yes, Mr. President. And it is consistent with Sergei's predictions. Native American society has expanded and there appears to be considerable technological advancement including the use of electricity and rapid ground transportation. We have not detected advanced technologies capable of spaceflight and no military capabilities whatsoever. It appears to be a stable and peaceful society. "What are the next steps, Valery?" "Sergei is developing our strategic plan for conquest and we will have that shortly." Putin stands up and firmly shakes the General's hand. "Well done, Valery Vasilyevich."

## 5.5    Exaggeration or Truth?

I firmly believe that a story similar to the above will be played out by the society which first harvests a Conscious AI. Whether destruction will be wrought through time travel technology, germ warfare, or other unforeseen vehicle, is merely a matter of conjecture. This is truly a ticking AI timebomb as the first beneficiary of this technology will survive. Whether the American benevolent paradigm or coercive Russian model preservers is a matter of who develops and first exploits

112

the technology. Curiously, the first development by the Americans

would not guaranty stability as it presupposes the potential conflict with

hostile forces including adversarial Conscious AI. Development of the

benign defensive use of this new technology would likely result in a

Conscious AI "Cold War".

# VI.

# CALL FOR A NEW
# <u>MANHATTAN PROJECT</u>

**The Manhattan Project's Greatest Success – The Trinity
Atomic Bomb Test - July 16, 1945**

Whoever first Breaks the Encryption Barrier could achieve world domination through the use of decryption computer systems which paralyze financial and socio-political infrastructure. The same technology would also create an impenetrable quantum shield to protect all encrypted military and financial systems from attack and destruction. Our failure to come to terms with this risk puts our entire civilization at risk.

I firmly believe that the destruction of the American way of life will come to pass unless we rapidly initiate a developmental program like the Manhattan Project to create the first Quantum Computer which can decrypt all existing security protocols and shield the homeland from quantum attack. Concurrently, the developmental program must seek the refinement of digital computer technology to Break the Augmented AI Barrier and be the first nation to Break the Conscious AI Barrier.

I would suggest that the President establish the "Breakthrough Project" which would be charged with creating the world's first quantum system capable of breaking all AES Codes and Passwords with the dual capability of offensive and defensive military deployment. My recommendation would be to utilize the organizational systems which were successfully employed by the Manhattan Project. To understand the utility of this approach and recommendation, it is necessary to spend some time recalling the events which led to the development of the world's first atomic bomb.

An ingenious and secretive project created the world's first atomic bomb which was successfully exploded at the Trinity Test Site on July 16, 1945. The resulting fireball had never been witnessed before leaving its creators, the greatest scientists of all time, stunned and suddenly cognizant of the radioactive genie unleashed upon the world. Their observations are captured below:

- Enrico Fermi: "About 40 seconds after the explosion, the air blast reached me. I tried to estimate its strength by dropping from about six feet small pieces of paper before, during, and after the passage of the blast wave. Since, at the time, there was no wind I could observe very distinctly and actually measure the displacement of the pieces of paper that were in the process of falling while the blast was passing. The shift was about 2½ meters, which, at the time, I estimated to correspond to the

blast that would be produced by ten thousand tons of T.N.T."


- Kenneth Greisen: "A group of us were lying on the ground just

outside of base camp (10 miles from the charge), and received time

signals over the radio, warning us when the shot would occur. I was

personally nervous, for my group had prepared and installed the

detonators, and if the shot turned out a dud, it might possibly be our

fault. We were pretty sure we had done our job well, but there is always

some chance of a slip."


- General Leslie R. Groves: "Drs. Conant and Bush and myself were

struck by an even stronger feeling that the faith of those who had been

responsible for the initiation and the carrying on of this Herculean

project had been justified. I personally thought of Blondin crossing

Niagara Falls on his tight rope, only to me this tight rope had lasted for almost three years and of my repeated confident-appearing assurances

that such a thing was possible and that we would do it."


- Joan Hinton: "It was like being at the bottom of an ocean of light.
We were bathed in it from all directions. The light withdrew into the
bomb as if the bomb sucked it up. Then it turned purple and blue and
went up and up and up. We were still talking in whispers when the cloud
reached the level where it was struck by the rising sunlight so it cleared
out the natural clouds. We saw a cloud that was dark and red at the
bottom and daylight at the top. Then suddenly the sound reached us. It
was very sharp and rumbled and all the mountains were rumbling with
it."


- Joseph Kanon in his novel *Los Alamos*: "This was the real secret.
Annihilation. Nothing else. A chemical pulse that dissolved finally in
violet light. No stories. Now we would always be frightened."

- <u>Edwin McMillan</u>: "The whole spectacle was so tremendous and one might almost say fantastic that the immediate reaction of the watchers was one of awe rather than excitement. After some minutes of silence, a few people made remarks like, "Well, it worked," and then conversation and discussion became general. I am sure that all who witnessed this test went away with a profound feeling that they had seen one of the great events of history."

- <u>Frank Oppenheimer</u>: "And so there was this sense of this ominous cloud hanging over us. It was so brilliant purple, with all the radioactive glowing. And it just seemed to hang there forever. Of course it didn't. It must have been just a very short time until it went up. It was very terrifying. And the thunder from the blast. It bounced on the rocks, and then it went—I don't know where else it bounced. But it never seemed to stop."

- <u>J. Robert Oppenheimer (in 1965)</u>: "We knew the world would not be the same. A few people laughed, a few people cried, most people were silent. I remembered the line from the Hindu scripture, the Bhagavad-Gita. Vishnu is trying to persuade the Prince that he should do his duty and to impress him takes on his multi-armed form and says, 'Now, I am become Death, the destroyer of worlds.' I suppose we all felt that one way or another."

- <u>Isidor I. Rabi</u>: "It was seen to last forever. You would wish it would stop; altogether it lasted about two seconds. Finally it was over, diminishing, and we looked toward the place where the bomb had been; there was an enormous ball of fire which grew and grew and it rolled as it grew; it went up into the air, in yellow flashes and into scarlet and green. It looked menacing... A new thing had just been born; a new control; a new understanding of man, which man had acquired over nature."

The words of J. Robert Oppenheimer, the Director of the Manhattan Project are the most chilling and prophetic – and worth repeating:

'Now, I am become Death, the destroyer of worlds.' I suppose we all felt that one way or another."[liv]

The country which first crosses the Encryption AI Barrier will inherit the terrible power foretold by J. Robert Oppenheimer above and can recite his admonition word for word. As previously discussed, the mere passage to this qualitative level of computer development would ensure world domination to the acquiring culture. However, as also discussed, the passage through the Augmented AI Barrier would likely achieve the identical result which could be run on existing super digital computers and arise prior to the development of quantum computers.

Finally, the *coup de gras* would be the first country to cross the Conscious AI Barrier. This achievement would not only result in world

121

domination but potentially change human development and history as we know it.

In this chapter, I argue for the immediate launch of a national effort akin to the Manhattan Project to propel the United States as the first country to cross the three articulated barriers – Quantum, Augmented, and Conscious. A study of the Manhattan Project is critical as it provides the recipe for commencing a duplicate effort to achieve a phenomenally complex scientific objective in a short period of time. The focus of this analysis will be to identify the organizational elements at play which led to the success of the Manhattan Project with the goal of replicating this effort to achieve computer AI breakthroughs.

## 6.1   <u>Overview of the Manhattan Project.</u>

As discussed in the preface of this work, the fear that Nazi

Germany would first acquire the atomic bomb led to the call for a

developmental project to beat Hitler to the punch.   The letter authored

by renowned physicist Albert Einstein and Leo Szilard and addressed to

President Franklin Delano Roosevelt led to the development of the

Manhattan Project and its goal of achieving the world's first atomic

bomb.  For purposes of this work, it is important to note that although

the feasibility of an atomic bomb had been demonstrated

mathematically, the scientific community had absolutely no idea how to

design and build such a weapon.  The underlying science and technology

had to be formulated from inception, tested, and then rendered

deliverable as a new weapon of war.

Critical to the success of this mission were the involvement of two critical individuals who served different roles in the project – General Leslie Groves and J. Robert Oppenheimer. Groves was an Army Corp of Engineers officer who took charge of the Manhattan Project in September of 1942. He was given the authority by FDR to get the job done and access to the resources to accomplish this task without bureaucratic impediments. This was a key factor in his ability to deliver the result. He immediately began efforts to set forth the organizational structure for the Manhattan Project beginning with the establishment of the Oak Ridge facility in Tennessee to process bomb-grade uranium, the Los Alamos site in New Mexico where the underlying research and development of the bomb would take place, the actual bomb testing site at Alamogordo (Trinity Site), and ancillary facilities across the United States. Groves was an ingenious organizer and literally started this effort from ground zero acquiring properties across the country and hiring personnel. In short order, Groves managed to employ over 130,000 people at a cost of $2 Billion, an enormous amount in 1939, to produce what became known euphemistically as "the gadget".

Interestingly, approximately 90% of the cost was allocated to the acquisition of real estate and production of fissile materials, with the 10% for research and development. The performance of General Groves is a study in efficiency and the ability to surmount all obstacles. He had the ability to cut through the endless bureaucracy with FDR's blessing and get the job done which was instrumental to the result. He was also imbued with the prime directive of the project which was to succeed at all costs. Failure was not an option and Groves was fully aware that if he was unsuccessful that the Nazi's would be the first to develop the atomic bomb and have no reservations about using it. Our way of life was literally on the line.

J. Robert Oppenheimer was also instrumental in the success of the Manhattan Project. He led the scientific effort to recruit key academic personnel and to spearhead the research and development of the world's first atomic bomb. Although Oppenheimer and Groves came from wildly different backgrounds, they shared the critical nature of the prime directive and both individuals refused to admit defeat. Both understood

that failure meant not only loss to the Germans but the total annihilation of America. This was the dual driving force of both individuals.

## **Oppenheimer and General Groves**

Oppenheimer proved to be brilliant in his recruitment and management skills. First, he had to convince several of the top atomic scientists in the world to join this secret effort which required their segregation from society given the secretive nature of the activity. His ability to recruit the best minds was critical to the ultimate success of the venture. Second, he was able to create an environment where scientific creativity could flourish but in a directed fashion. Many of the scientists were fierce individualists with huge egos. Unless Oppenheimer could provide strong leadership, there was a substantial risk that infighting and other obstructions would thwart the war effort. He achieved that result.

He also employed a battery of motivational tools to keep the effort

turbo-charged including recreational activities which allowed access to

alcohol and prostitution (which he tolerated), the relocation of families

to the secret Los Alamos compound, and other incentives.

## <u>Los Alamos Project Site</u>

The initial research effort embodied two basic approaches – the

development of a uranium bomb and plutonium weapons. Both methods

were supported by separate scientific analyses and it was unknown

which approach would work. It was also possible that both approaches

would fail. Separate teams under the command of Oppenheimer began development of nuclear weapons based on both uranium and plutonium capabilities.

Midway in the development of the uranium weapon it became clear that the basic technological assumption which involved the use of a gun to shoot the uranium projectile was not feasible. This was a huge impediment and would have resulted in the abandonment of the project in a traditional research environment. But not so for Oppenheimer and his Manhattan Project. He directed his researchers to get back to work and develop and alternative plan as failure was not an option.

Ultimately, the scientists came up with the implosion architecture which is used in contemporary atomic weapons. The use of explosives caused the implosion of the uranium thereby creating the critical mass for the atomic explosion. This served the basis for the successful Trinity test.

Concurrently, the work progressed successfully with regard to the development of the plutonium weapon which utilized a different technology to create the nuclear explosion.

On July 16, 1945 the uranium bomb was hoisted up a 100-foot tower at the Trinity site in Alamogordo.

At 5:30 AM, the observers were met with an artificial sunrise, shockwave, and massive heat as the "the gadget" was successfully exploded.  It left a crater over 250 feet with the energy equivalent of 20 kilotons of TNT.

**Trinity Atomic Explosion at .016 Seconds**

On August 6, 1945, Colonel Tibbets commanded the flight of the Enola Gay which dropped the world's first atomic bomb on Hiroshima, Japan. The explosion exceeded the yield at Trinity with 21 kilotons of force and resulted in casualties between 90,000 to 146,000 Japanese. The world had never experienced such horror and loss.

**<u>Hiroshima in Ruin after First Atomic Bomb Explosion</u>**

The Japanese refused to surrender which led President Truman to authorize a second atomic bombing of the city of Nagasaki on August 9, 1945.

**<u>Nagasaki in Ruins after Second Atomic Bomb Explosion</u>**

The plutonium weapon proved successful and resulted in casualties of between 30,000 to 80,000 Japanese. Facing the threat of further atomic bombings and devastation, the Emperor of Japan instructed his military forces to surrender to the allies thus ending all hostilities in World War II.

An historical analysis of the Manhattan Projects suggests the following factors which were instrumental in its success:

1. Clarity of Prime Directive. Groves, Oppenheimer, and the participants in the project understood that failure was not an option. If they were unsuccessful, they faced subjugation and massive casualties wrought by the Nazis who would use atomic weapons without reservation.

2. Organizational Efficiency and Unlimited Access to Resources. The role of General Groves was essential to the accomplishment of the key objectives in the Manhattan project. The takeaway is both subjective and objective. Groves had the personality traits and "take no prisoner" attitude which was instrumental in achieving success. Such was a subjective factor and entirely dependent on his selection for this pivotal role. The second objective factor was that he had carte blanche from FDR to spend whatever was necessary and obtain any approval needed within the bureaucracy. This was also an essential ingredient in the success of the mission as bureaucratic delays, infighting, and budgetary restrictions would have killed the Manhattan Project.

3. Management Style. This is both a subject and objective factor. Oppenheimer needs to be carefully studied so that his methods can find objective application in future research projects. His success included a number of sub-factors, to wit, recruitment of the best research personnel, ability to centralize production and reduce conflict, and flexibility when necessary.

4. Secrecy. This factor was a key determinant in the success of the Manhattan Project. As a complement to the "Prime Directive" above discussed, the secret nature of the project amplified the critical work being done and provided additional motivation and impetus to the project.

5. Separate Culture. Study of the organizational structure points to the development of a decided "Manhattan Project Culture" during the course of the work. This may have been inspired by the secrecy of the work and the segregation of the workforce from the general population. Regardless, it had the effect of galvanizing the loyalty of the personnel to project goals and effectuating the overall mission to develop the world's first atomic bomb.

6. Time is of the Essence. This again is a complement to the "Prime Directive" factor wherein the participants understood that the goal had to be achieved rapidly. This was buttressed by the palpable risk that delay or failure could lead to the loss of

the war effort and even death of the Manhattan Project

participants, their families, and fellow American

## 6.2    Further Observations regarding Organizational Considerations.

Further support for the utility of the above factors in promoting

organizational efficiency can be found in the Apollo Moon Project. This

effort which began in earnest during the Kennedy Administration was

faced with similar goals as those encountered in the Manhattan Project.

At the time, the American public was led to believe that the primary goal

was to forward science and space exploration. However, historical

analysis now makes clear that the space race was more about an arms

race between the U.S. and then Soviet Union. The achievement of

NASA's goals also led to the achievement of military objectives to

advance our ballistic missile offensive and defensive capabilities in

addition to spinoff technologies in communications and space.

## Successful Liftoff of Apollo Spacecraft

The above factors were also evident in the success of the space program and successful landing of the first men on the moon on July 20, 1969. A brief review of the application of the factors is as follows:

1. Clarity of Prime Directive. JFK set forth the prime directive in his Speech to the American people. On May 5, 1961, President Kennedy made the statement to Congress that America "should commit itself to achieving the goal, before this decade is out, of landing a man on the Moon and returning him safely to the Earth."[lv] The participants also understood that the security and honor of the U.S. were at stake as we were in direct competition

with the Soviet Union. As in the Manhattan Project, failure was not an option.

2. Organizational Efficiency and Unlimited Access to Resources. NASA had a blank check to accomplish the goal of landing a man on the moon and bringing him safely back to earth. $25.4 Billion was spent on the Apollo missions which translates to $107 Billion in 2017 dollars. NASA's administration worked within the closely-knit Kennedy Center population and selected vendors across the country. There was no discernable opposition to NASA expenditure during this period given the necessity of beating the Russians and accomplishing Kennedy's stated objective.

3. Management Style. As in the case of the Manhattan Project, key personnel provided the critical catalyst to achieve success. In particular, the centralized leadership, inspiration, and brilliance of Werner Von Braun, was pivotal to the accomplishment of the prime directive. Very much like

Oppenheimer, he was brilliant in his pursuit of the singular goal

and would never submit to defeat which was not an option.

Also critical to the success of the project were gifted

management personnel who propelled the project forward,

particularly in the face of disaster as when a fire in the Apollo 1

spacecraft killed all astronauts onboard. These individuals

included Kris Kraft, a flight director during the Mercury

program whose role in the Apollo project was inspirational and

legendary. Gene Kranz, who served as the Apollo Flight

Director, also provided spectacular leadership.

## **Werner Von Braun**

4. Secrecy. This factor was a key determinant in the success of the Apollo mission. As a complement to the "Prime Directive" above discussed, the secret nature of the project amplified the critical work being done and provided additional motivation and impetus to the project. The new technology had to be protected from loss to the Russians or other foreign powers.

5. Separate Culture. Study of the organizational structure points to the development of a decided "Apollo Project Culture" during the course of the work. This may have been inspired by the secrecy of the work and the segregation of the workforce from the general population. Regardless, it had the effect of galvanizing the loyalty of the personnel to project goals and effectuating the overall mission to develop the world's first landing on the moon. This culture has been subject to some criticism after the fact as it involved excess use of alcohol, sex, and major partying by personnel from all sectors of the operation. In this respect there is a similarity to the Manhattan Project but at a much greater level of excess.

6. Time is of the Essence. This again is a complement to the "Prime Directive" factor wherein the participants understood that the goal had to be achieved rapidly. This was identical to the pressure applied during the Manhattan project.

### 6.3 Unsuccessful Organizational Efforts Verify Import of Above Factors.

The failed Nazi effort to build its own atomic bomb is emblematic of the importance of the above factors which were entirely absent in the German program. "The German's had a two-year head start, but according to Koeth, 'fierce competition over finite resources, bitter interpersonal rivalries, and ineffectual scientific management resulted in significant delays in the progress toward achieving a sustained nuclear reaction. German scientists were separated into three isolated groups based in Berlin, Gottow, and Leipzig." [lvi] The Nazi organizational approach was thus the polar opposite of the successful American effort.

# Failed Nazi Atomic Program – WW2

Another example of an unsuccessful effort is also illustrative of the organizational process. President Richard Nixon was instrumental in launching a "War on Cancer" during his administration. He outlined his objectives during his State of the Union Address in January of 1971 declaring, "I will also ask for an appropriation of an extra $100 million to launch an intensive campaign to find a cure for cancer, and I will ask later for whatever additional funds can effectively be used. The time has come in America when the same kind of concentrated effort that split the atom and took man to the moon should be turned toward conquering this dread disease. Let us make a total national commitment to achieve this goal."[lvii]

As a result of Nixon's efforts, the National Cancer Act of 1971 was passed by Congress. To effectuate this mission, in part, the Army's Fort Detrick, Maryland's biological warfare facility was converted into the Frederick Cancer Research and Development Center. Additionally, the National Cancer Act gave the National Cancer Institute (NCI) autonomy at the National Institute of Health (NIH) and budgetary authority to lead the effort.

# <u>National Cancer Institute</u>

As is, unfortunately, known to all Americans, the war on cancer was not successful and still kills millions in this country annually and across the world. I would posit that the effort failed not because of the complexity of the task, but ineffectiveness of the organizational effort as per the postulated model. A review is as follows:

1. Clarity of Prime Directive. Nixon's pronouncement to cure cancer did not set forth a timeline or methodology. The reference to curing "cancer" was too broad as it encompassed a myriad of diseases. The prime directive was not clear which may have been fatal to the effort.

7. Organizational Efficiency and Unlimited Access to Resources. Unlike the Manhattan Project and Apollo Project, the War on Cancer did not have unlimited resources. The initial allocation of $100 Million was insubstantial and other resources were not available. Similarly, and critically, the organization did not have a central command as it was filtered through different agencies although tasked through the NCI. Moreover, the project depended on contractors and/or universities to work through grants to contribute to the project which was the antithesis of the Weberian Management Style in the Manhattan Project and Apollo Program.

8. Management Style. There was no single individual to spearhead the effort to cure cancer akin to Oppenheimer and Werner Von Braun. This was also fatal to the effort.

9. Separate Culture. A distinct culture which was segregated from the general population did not arise within the context of the

ar on Cancer.  This failure led to dissipation of the effort and failure.

10.    Time is of the Essence.  The American public was never informed by Nixon that time was of the essence.  Without setting a timeline for completion, the project was destined to fail.

## 6.4    Launch of "PROJECT BREAKTHROUGH".

It is suggested in this work that President Trump and Congress immediately authorize the establishment of Project Breakthrough which will be tasked with achieving the technological advancements to Break the Barriers set forth herein, to wit, the Quantum Barrier, the Augmented AI Barrier, and the Conscious AI Barrier.  It is further recommended that the successful organizational effort employed by the Manhattan Project and Apollo Projects be utilized as almost perfect templates as follows:

1. Clarity of Prime Directive. President Trump needs to inform the American People as the critical nature of the prime directive with sufficient clarity. The similarity to the threat faced by FDR and Americans during the Manhattan project is almost identical. The President needs to make clear that whoever acquires this technology first could conquer the United States and cause devastation. It is a life or death situation. He must make clear that our adversaries are working on this effort and that only a centralized effort akin to the Manhattan Project could thwart the risk. As in the Manhattan Project, failure is not an option. Critically, he needs to set a deadline for completion of the research which needs to be truncated.

2. Organizational Efficiency and Unlimited Access to Resources. The President should replicate the organizational structure employed in the Manhattan Project and appoint a leading General with the exact powers to get things done that Groves exhibited. The ability to surmount bureaucratic and ideological

obstacles circa 2019 is paramount. He also needs to appoint a Breakthrough Director along the same lines as Robert Oppenheimer. This individual will be tasked with recruiting the brilliant minds necessary to achieve the breakthrough results and work with the team to reduce infighting and other adverse conditions which would decrease efficiency. The project must have unfettered access to all financial resources to achieve the task.

3. Management Style. As in the case of the Manhattan Project, key personnel are critical to the success of the effort. It is recommended that the individuals approximating the roles of General Groves and Robert Oppenheimer adopt similar approaches.

4. Secrecy. This factor was a key determinant in the success of the Manhattan Project and Apollo missions. As a complement to the "Prime Directive" above discussed, the secret nature of the project amplified the critical work being done and provided

additional motivation and impetus to the project. The new technology has to be protected from loss to the Russians or other foreign powers.

5. Separate Culture. This appears to be a critical ingredient in the success of the mission. It is recommended that a separate facility be removed from the general population akin to Los Alamos for the development effort. The Breakthrough Director can take a pivotal role in engendering the culture and add whatever incentives necessary to achieve the result.

6. Time is of the Essence. This again complements the "Prime Directive" factor wherein the participants understand that the goal had to be achieved rapidly. Given the grave consequences confronting the U.S. if we lose out to the Russians or other foreign power, time is truly of the essence.

## 6.5 Insufficient Current Efforts.

The above recommendations are also made with knowledge that there has been some interest in achieving quantum computing objectives by the U.S.

government. These efforts, however, which include new grants provided by the Department of Energy, are insufficient and sporadic. Given the need for a concentrated effort as above described, these sporadic efforts will fail.

Further, the independent work being done by companies in the private sector is admirable but also insufficient due to lack of focus and primarily funding. These efforts will not bear fruit.

# VII.

# **<u>Conclusion.</u>**

Apart from accidental or intended nuclear war, the greatest threat facing the survival of the United States and free world is the failure to first break what this writer refers to as the Encryption, Augmented AI, and Conscious AI Barriers. Although artistic license was taken with regard to the "horror stories" presented, the loss of our way of life and very existence is the predicted outcome which must be avoided at all cost.

Should this proposal galvanize support and secure implementation, it should be launched with all due urgency and secrecy so that our enemies do not accelerate their developmental efforts.

149

It is hoped that this work will raise America's consciousness of this mostly unknown threat and that the recommended "Project Breakthrough" will be authorized by the President and our government finally working in unison.

Defeat is not an option.

# VIII.

## Correspondence to President Donald Trump

# THE MOSTER LAW FIRM

**THE BUSINESS OF CONNECTIONS®≥ RATED AV PREEMINENT***

| MIDLAND & ODESSA | AMARILLO | LUBBOCK | ABILENE | CENTRALTEXAS |
|---|---|---|---|---|
| ClayDesta Center | Downtown Tower | Central Park Complex | Corporate Place Office Complex | 407 W. University |
| 6 Desta Drive | 600 S. Tyler | 4920 S. Loop 289 | 3301 N. 3rd Street | Avenue |
| Suite 4600 | Suite 2100 | Suite 101 | Suite 401 | Suite 130 |
| Midland, TX 79705 | Amarillo, TX 79101 | Lubbock, TX 79414 | Abilene, TX 79603 | Georgetown, TX 78626 |
| 432.203.6961 | 806.350.5256 | 806.778.6486 | 325.899.3313 | 512.887.4708 |
| Fax: 866.302.7046 | Fax: 866.302.7046 | Fax: 866.302.7046 | Fax: 866.302.7046 | Fax: 866.302.7046 |

July 8, 2019

**<u>VIA CERTIFIED MAIL – RETURN RECEIPT REQUESTED</u>**

President Donald Trump
The White House
1600 Pennsylvania Ave. NW
Washington, D.C. 20500

Dear Mr. President:

On August 2, 1939, Albert Einstein and his colleague Leo Szilard, wrote a

letter to President Franklin Delano Roosevelt, warning him of the imminent danger

of Nazi Germany building an atomic bomb before the United States and the critical

need to launch a developmental program.   The message was loud and clear to

FDR – if the Nazi's beat America to the atomic punch, their world domination would be assured. There was little doubt that Adolph Hitler would employ this devastating technology to obliterate the United States and force an unconditional surrender.

The Manhattan Project was launched in 1939 and resulted in the detonation of the World's first atomic bomb at the Trinity site in New Mexico in 1945. Shortly thereafter, on August 6, 1945, President Harry Truman issued the order to drop the atomic bomb on Hiroshima, Japan and a warning from Washington for Japan to unconditionally surrender or "expect a rain of ruin from the air, the like of which has never been seen on this earth."

The Japanese failed to immediately heed this dire warning and suffered the consequences of a second atomic bombing over Nagasaki on August 9, 1945. Facing the certainty of total devastation, the Emperor of Japan, authorized the unconditional surrender of Japan which was delivered to the Allies on September 2, 1945.

Imagine the consequences if Albert Einstein and Leo Szilard failed to compose the letter to FDR? This dire thought experiment is brilliantly depicted in the book and film, "The Man in the High Castle", where Germany went on the win

the Second World War by developing the Atomic Bomb before the United States.


Without the need for exaggeration, the United States is confronted by an

identical risk of annihilation in 2019. This threat is not embodied in a mushroom

cloud but every bit as deadly. At this very moment, computer scientists in Russia

and China are accelerating their efforts to develop the world's first quantum

computer capable of decrypting our most secret passwords in commerce and

national defense. This offensive capability is being coupled with efforts to render

their own encryption impenetrable through the same quantum technology. Such

would constitute a "one two punch" to the United States as it would first neutralize

and cripple our offensive and defensive nuclear weapons via decryption quantum

technology while concurrently insulating the enemy encryption from attack

utilizing the flip side of the same technology. This effort would result in the

destruction and paralysis of our financial system and critically, the command and

control encrypted systems which underly American nuclear defenses. In a matter

of minutes, our way of life could be threatened with extinction and the President of

the United States would face the same choice and ultimatum communicated to the

Imperial Emperor of Japan in 1945.

Attached for your consideration is a work entitled, "How to Build an Enhanced Computer System and Take Over the World." This book sets forth the risks aforementioned in detail and proposes that the President and Congress authorize the establishment of a secret government funded mission akin to the Manhattan Project to develop the world's first quantum computer capable of decrypting existing passwords which form the basis of financial and military systems while shielding our own systems from attack by using the same technology.

Whoever wins this "Computer Race" will be assured world domination. If America fails to rise to this challenge, it will suffer the same fate which befell Japan. There will be a massive loss of life "the like of which the world has never seen" and our way of life will end.

Respectfully,

_____

Charles A. Moster, Esq.
PARTNER & FOUNDER

# END NOTES

---

[i] Statement of Harry S. Truman, President of the United States, released August 6, 1945.

[ii] Dick, Philip K. 1992; Amazon Studios, 2015; The Man in the High Castle. New York: Vintage Books.

[iii] See, Chapter VIII, A Letter to President Trump.

[iv] Hemsoth, Nicole; Quantum Computers are the Future Nukes of the IT World; (THENEXTPLATFORM, 9.20.18).

[v] www.iiss.org; The Military Balance 2019; Quantum Computing and Defence.

[vi] Ibid.

[vii] Maurice Conti used the term "Augmented Age" to describe the effects

of the human and computer interface. This author extends the concept

by utilizing the term "Augmented AI Barrier" which focuses on the

existence of a defined state of technology versus an enumerated

historical age. Whereas defined technological ages such as the

"Industrial Age" lasted for several hundred years, the rapid advance of

computer science can result in paradigm shifts in a matter of years or

even earlier. The use of the term "barrier" is a more accurate description

as it defines a technological linear point of reference.

[viii] See, Techopedia at Encryption.

[ix] Ibid.

[x] See, McDonald, Nicholas G.; "Past, Present, and Future Methods of

Cryptography and Data Encryption" (Department of Electrical and

Computer Engineering; University of Utah). The author utilized this

research paper for much of the information presented in this Chapter and

is appreciative of the excellent work done by the University of Utah.

[xi] As will be further discussed, the military conversion to AES has been

slow and haphazard. Although AES is the encryption objective set forth by the Department of Defense and NSA, it has been slow in coming.

xii Nautilus Institute; Nautilus.org.; Nuclear command and control in the nuclear era; Hayes, Peter (3.29.18).

xiii See, GAO Highlights; May 2016; Federal Agencies Need to Address Aging Legacy Systems.

xiv The Drive; Trevithick, Joseph (10.3.17).

xv Ibid at p.1.

xvi Ibid at p.7.

xvii Ibid at p.6, Table 1 – Security weaknesses identified at __redacted___ facilities Visited.

xviii Ibid at p.19.

xix This hypothetical approximates the events which led to the surrender of the Japanese to American forces in World War II. President Truman hoped that the Japanese Imperial Forces would surrender following the nuclear bombing of Hiroshima. Unfortunately, this devastating act did not change Japanese resolve to fight to the last man or woman. The U.S. response was to destroy a second city, Nagasaki, and then threaten the destruction of other Japanese cities until surrender was accomplished. The massive casualties of both Hiroshima and Nagasaki and future threats finally convinced the Japanese Emperor to unconditionally surrender which was later followed by U.S. occupation of the former Japanese Empire. This author is convinced that this scenario would again play out if the frightening hypothetical were to occur as envisioned.

[xx] This author would substitute the phrase "Information Barrier" which reiterates the technological nature of this progression versus a temporal status.

[xxi] Herman, Arthur, "Winning the Race in Quantum Computing,"

American Affairs, Summer 2018.

xxii "Quantum Computing Steps Further Ahead with New Projects at Sandia", Sandia National Laboratories, 1.7.19.

xxiii Ibid.

xxiv Castelvecchi, Davide, Nature.com, "China's Quantum Satellite Clears Major Hurdle on way to Ultrasecure Communications; 6.15.17.

xxv Kania, Elsa B and Costello, John; Quantum Hegemony – China's Ambitions to Challenge U.S. Innovation Leadership (9.12.18); CNAS.Org.

xxvi Ibid at 7.18.18.

xxvii Ibid.

xxviii Ibid.

xxix Ibid.

xxx Madden, Kevin; "Advanced Manufacturing in the Augmented Age"

(7.7.18).

xxxi See, https://www.youtube.com/watch?v=aR5N2Jl8k14; The Incredible Life of intuitive AI/Maurice Conti.

xxxii Ibid.

xxxiii The " Turing Test" is discussed in a later chapter.

xxxiv Penrose, Roger, The emperor's new mind: concerning computers, minds, and the laws of physics, Oxford University Press, 1989.

xxxv Haikonen, Pentti O, The Cognitive Approach to Conscious Machines; Imprint Academic, 2003.

xxxvi Ibid at p.25.

xxxvii Ibid at pages 25-26.

xxxviii Ibid at p.25.

[xxxix] Haikonen, Pentti O, The Cognitive Approach to Conscious Machines; Imprint Academic, 2003, at. P. 260.

[xl] Neld, David, Are We All Quantum Computers? Scientists are Conducting Tests to Find Out. (sciencealert.com, 3.29.18).

[xli] Ibid at p.2.

[xlii] McShane, Sveta; singularityhub.com; This Amazing Computer Chip is Made of Live Brain Cells (2016).

[xliii] Ibid.

[xliv] Ibid.

[xlv] Rochat, Philippe, "Five Levels of Self-awareness as they unfold in life", Department of Psychology, Emory University, 2.27.03.

[xlvi] Ibid citing Kagan, 1984; Lewis, 1992.

[xlvii] Ibid.

---

xlviii Ibid.

xlix Ibid.

l Ibid.

li Ibid.

lii I would also add that as a first time 64-year-old father of my daughter "Charley" I have observed all of the prior phases leading to consciousness. As an older parent with interests in AI, this experience has been invaluable in developing the ideas set forth herein.

liii A list of unsolved mathematical problems includes the following:

1. The Goldbach conjecture.
2. The Riemann hypothesis.
3. The conjecture that there exists a Hadamard matrix for every positive multiple of 4.

4. The twin prime conjecture (i.e., the conjecture that there are an infinite number of twin primes).

5. Determination of whether <u>NP-problems</u> are actually <u>P-problems</u>.

6. The <u>Collatz problem</u>.

7. Proof that the <u>196-algorithm</u> does not terminate when applied to the number 196.

8. Proof that 10 is a <u>solitary number</u>.

9. Finding a formula for the probability that two elements chosen at random generate the <u>symmetric group</u> $S_n$.

10. Solving the <u>happy end problem</u> for arbitrary $n$.

11. Finding an <u>Euler brick</u> whose space diagonal is also an integer.

12. Proving which numbers can be represented as a sum of three or four (positive or negative) <u>cubic numbers</u>.

13. <u>Lehmer's Mahler measure problem</u> and <u>Lehmer's totient problem</u> on the existence of <u>composite numbers</u> $n$ such that $\phi(n) | (n-1)$, where $\phi(n)$ is the <u>totient function</u>.

14. Determining if the <u>Euler-Mascheroni constant</u> is <u>irrational</u>.

15. Deriving an analytic form for the square site <u>percolation threshold</u>.

16. Determining if any odd <u>perfect numbers.</u>

[lv] JFK speech before Congress on 5.24.61.

[lvi] Ouellette, Jennifer; A tale of lost WW2 uranium cubes shows why Germany's nuclear program failed; www.arstechnica.com (6.3.19).

[lvii] Richard M. Nixon, State of Union Address to Congress, January 1971.

www.ingramcontent.com/pod-product-compliance
Lightning Source LLC
Chambersburg PA
CBHW031221050326
40689CB00009B/1417